A HISTORY OF FURTHER EDUCATION IN HULL

Written, researched and compiled by Robert Barnard for the Local History Unit
Unit supervised by Christopher Ketchell

1996

Published jointly by the Hutton Press Ltd.,
130 Canada Drive, Cherry Burton,
Beverley, East Yorkshire HU17 7SB

and Hull College

CONTENTS

ACKNOWLEDGEMENTS

I would like to thank the staff of the Hull Local Studies Library and Kingston upon Hull Records Office for their invaluable assistance.

Hull College for access to archive material and illustrations. Robb Robinson for proof reading

The University of Hull for permission to quote from Mr Mitchell's thesis on Hull College of Technology.

The following abbreviations have been used in illustration credits: RB - Robert Barnard, HC - Hull College, RH - Richard Hayton, HCM - Hull City Museums and Art Galleries, CJK - Christopher Ketchell, RS - Robert Strafford, KHRO - Hull City Record Office.

ROBERT BARNARD
Local History Unit
Hull College
Park Street Centre

December 1996

PREFACE

Welcome to Robert Barnard's history of Hull College. I was very pleased to be asked to write a short preface celebrating our first hundred years and to express my thanks to Robert for his attention to the detail of the College's development and his evocation of the characters and personalities of Hull's famous citizens.

About ten percent of Hull residents attend the College each year, so yours would be a rare family if one of your relatives had not enrolled for Women's Industry Courses (1890s) or Public Health (1900s) or Aeronautical Engineering (1940s) or Flour Milling (1950s) or Business Studies or Building or Engineering or Computing. You will see more than a little of Hull's history in this story of the College's growth and change. I hope, like me, you will find something to entertain you, something to learn, and something to admire in Hull's people's determination to acquire new skills to improve the city and their situation.

There are few Further Education or Technical colleges that can trace their roots back a hundred years. There are few in England that have more students than Hull College. We need, I think, that history and that size to help us provide for the citizens of Hull the quality and diversity of educational opportunities that will be needed over the next one hundred years. Your children and grandchildren will as students or members of staff, I hope, make the coming years as exciting and as successful as those you will read about in this history.

Hull College is proud to serve the City of Kingston-upon-Hull - long may it continue to do so.

Peter Moseley
Principal of Hull College

ORIGINS OF TECHNICAL EDUCATION

Education for all is a relatively recent idea and before the late nineteenth century most schools only taught a small but influential section of the population. The churches dominated the provision of schools during the nineteenth century but opposed general education and the policy of the Anglican National Society was clearly stated in 1805 by Dr Bell. *"It is not proposed that the children of the poor be educated in an expensive manner, or even taught to write and cipher ... There is a risk of elevating, by an indiscriminate education, the minds of those doomed to the drudgery of daily labour above their conditions, and thereby rendering them discontented and unhappy in their lot."* These attitudes conflicted strongly with the German Lutheran Church's emphasis on the value of educating the majority, which was to give Continental Europe a head start when the demand for technical education increased later in the century.

During the first half of the nineteenth century the general view prevailed that Great Britain owed her success to national characteristics and qualities and that craftsmen were endowed with natural abilities; non-academic education had little purpose. Self improvement and self help were seen as the keys to prosperity; a Chancellor of the Exchequer even stated that *"I hold it as a duty not to spend money to do that which people can do for themselves."*[1]

The need for technical education sprang from the industrial revolution, which gradually replaced the artisan in his workshop. However the pioneers of the industrial revolution were untutored 'self-made men' who had gained little from education systems. Industry grew unplanned with social squalor, undeveloped state action and rudimentary child education but there was also immense inventive and scientific progress. To operate new machinery the industrial workers required some specialised education that would make them more effective employees. However they were not to be educated *"above their class"*[2], but would merely be provided with sufficient to enable them to do their duty more efficiently.

HULL'S EARLY TECHNICAL EDUCATION

Towards the end of the eighteenth century there was a rapid expansion of educational facilities in Hull. Sunday Schools, day schools and a spinning school all helped to discipline the 'lower orders' and increase the supply of trained servants. The growth of educational facilities coincided with the town's greatest period of economic expansion, which inevitably changed its character both politically and socially. Industry became stimulated by Hull's growth as a port, the principal industries of the late eighteenth and early nineteenth centuries being shipbuilding and the processing of some of the raw materials that came into the port. By 1818 there were a wide range of industrial establishments including eleven corn mills, two sugar houses, two oil mills, a whiting mill, two lead mills, a glue factory, a soapery, a foundry, an engine manufactory, six roperies and manufactories for making sailcloth and spinning woollen yarns. Most of these industries provided only seasonal employment.

Fig. 1. Trinity House Navigation School (The Graphic, 11.3.1882)

By 1835 Hull was no longer a rather conservative seaport but one of the main doors to the rapidly growing 'workshop of the world'. The social changes caused by the coming of the new industrial society could scarcely fail to leave their impact upon Hull.

The Hull Trinity House, which controlled navigation in the port, had paid for navigation classes from at least 1729; this was probably the first 'organised' technical education in Hull. In 1785 they founded the Trinity House Navigation School in Trinity House Lane. The boys were taught navigation, arithmetic, writing, accounts and practical religion. Initially the school reputedly suffered from ill-discipline and low standards, however, by the turn of the century conditions improved. It moved in 1842, reorganised and enlarged in 1849 and by 1856 had 98 boys. From the early 1850s it received Government grants from the Science and Art Department, South Kensington, for teaching navigation and in 1872 added an adult department to prepare seamen for master's certificates.

During the late eighteenth century many private academies for the middle classes appeared in Hull, usually in the proprietor's own house. They provided some technical and commercial as well as academic education although usually at a very elementary level. The most significant of these schools, Snowden's Mercantile Academy in Blanket Row existed for nearly half a century. Snowden's offered courses for boys *"intended for the accounting-house"* and *"practical mathematics, particularly navigation and surveying"*.[3] Classes for girls took place in a separate apartment. Some retired seafarers also offered technical classes.

From 1795 winter classes for young sailors were recorded at an unidentified school started by subscription. The following year 170 boys were admitted and when the school closed after 1808 there were 89 boys registered.

Hull's parents seemed to appreciate the value of education. One woman remarked on schools that used older pupils as monitors, *"I don't like them, because lads teach, and then they say to t'others, 'If you won't gie me summut, i'll have you afore th' maister'; and them as can afford to gie 'em summut does well enough, and them as can't, doesn't do no good".*[4]

Occasionally middle class parents objected to education being carried beyond reading, writing and arithmetic. A respectable Hull woman stated that she had not allowed her daughters to learn to write *"because it would only set them writing love letters".*[5]

Hull's foremost physician, Dr Alderson, attempted to found a commercial college in 1802 but unfortunately the scheme never came to fruition. The Hull Subscription Library held scientific and literary meetings from 1803 and from 1804 there were annual lecture courses in scientific and commercial subjects. When the Literary and Philosophical Society was formed in 1822 it took over some of the lecture courses from the Subscription Library although these benefited mainly middle class adults. The Subscription Library and the Literary and Philosophical Society built the Royal Institution in Albion Street as a joint centre in 1853.

Mechanics Institutes became established from 1823 to *"instruct artisans in the scientific principles of arts and mathematics".*[6] Hull Mechanics Institute was founded in 1825 its aim being, *"the instruction of its members, at a cheap rate, in the principles of their respective arts, and in the various branches of science and useful knowledge".*[7] It provided winter courses of lectures in natural and experimental philosophy, practical mechanics, astronomy, chemistry, literature and the arts. By the 1850s its facilities included a library, reading room and news room, lecture hall, museum and model room. In 1857 there were 115 honorary members, 520 proprietary members, 185 apprentice members and 6 women members. By 1850 there were some 610 institutes nationally with 102,050 members. Unfortunately, the students received little benefit from any technical instruction given because they lacked sufficient elementary education to cope with the necessary theoretical work.

Membership of Mechanics Institutes increasingly consisted more of clerks, apprentices and

Fig. 2. The Mechanics Institute, Charlotte Street (Greenwood's Picture of Hull, 1835)

middle class people than working men. In Hull 'operative mechanics and labourers' were admitted to lectures in 1857, but not the reading room. The syllabuses also gradually altered with reduced technical instruction but after the early 1860s the Hull Mechanics Institute contributed little educationally. Mechanics Institutes also failed due to inappropriate teaching methods and a lack of competent teachers.

Numerous other organisations also provided some form of local technical education. The Hull YMCA started in 1847 and a mutual improvement society met in Bowlalley Lane in 1853. The Church Institute, founded in 1845, aimed *"to promote the study of literature and science ... in subordination to religion"*.[8] It moved in 1865 to Dr Alderson's former house in Albion Street and at the time had about 650 members. With similar aims but without denominational attachments, the Young People's Christian and Literary Institute was founded in 1860. This replaced the Mechanics Institute with popular adult evening classes and after 1869 became a vigorous centre of science teaching under the Science and Art Department, as also on a

smaller scale did the Church Institute after 1872. Adults with little elementary education were partially catered for in the 1850s and 1860s by some parish clergy in National Schools. After 1870 the Friends' Adult School in Mason Street became important, with one of the largest attendanc's in Yorkshire.

Even by 1865 only 250 Hull boys, mainly middle class, out of a total population of 120 000 were receiving secondary education. By national standards this figure was scandalously low. J. Lawson has commented that Hull's middle class answered closely Matthew Arnold's description of the English Philistines - predominantly nonconformist tradesmen, self made, self reliant, self satisfied.

Fig. 3. The Royal Institution, Albion Street. The sketch also shows the Art School to the left of the Institution and what was to become the Commercial Department and Offices of the Hull Municipal Technical School at 7 Albion Street on the right (HCM)

HULL LITERARY AND PHILOSOPHICAL SOCIETY.

FOUNDED IN 1822.

ROYAL INSTITUTION, ALBION-STREET.

LIST OF MEETINGS DURING THE SESSION 1893-94.

THE DOORS WILL BE OPENED ONE HOUR BEFORE EACH AFTERNOON OR EVENING LECTURE.

DATE.	LECTURER.	SUBJECT.
1893.		
1..Oct. 31st, 8 p.m.	Professor W. M. FLINDERS PETRIE, D.C.L., Author of "Pyramids and Temples of Gizeh," "Stonehenge," &c..	PRIMITIVE EGYPT. Lantern Illustrations.
2..Nov. 14th, 7.30 p.m.	CONVERSAZIONE.	
3..Nov. 28th, 8 p.m. ...	WALTER MACFARREN, Esq., Professor and Fellow of the Royal Academy of Music..............	RECITAL LECTURE :—The Pianoforte and Pianoforte Composers.
4..Dec. 5th, 8 p.m.	W. BOYD DAWKINS, Esq., M.A., F.R.S., F.S.A., Professor of Geology at Owens College, Manchester ; Author of "Cave Hunting," "Early Man in Britain," &c..	A PRIMEVAL FOREST. Lantern Illustrations.
5..Dec. 19th, 8 p.m......	Professor L. C. MIALL, F.R.S.	LIFE AT THE SURFACE OF THE WATER. The experiments will be shown by Stroud and Rendell's Lantern.
1894.		
6..Jan. 2nd, 8 p.m.	J. WELLS, Esq., M.A., Fellow and Tutor of Wadham College, Oxford	HISTORY OF OXFORD. Lantern Illustrations.
7..Jan. 16th, 8 p.m....	ALFRED H. ALLEN, Esq., F.C.S., of Sheffield	EYES AND DYES—A Discourse on Colour Vision. Illustrated with Experiments.
8..Jan. 30th, 8 p.m.....	DOUGLAS FRESHFIELD, Esq., President of the Alpine Club, and Honorary Secretary of the Royal Geographical Society...........	THE DISCOVERY OF THE ALPS. Lantern Illustrations.
9..Feb. 13th, 8 p.m.	Miss EDITH TULLOCH, Soprano..... Miss DORA TULLOCH, Reciter ..... Miss BERYL TULLOCH, Mandolin... Miss ADA TULLOCH, Guitar	POETIC AND MUSICAL RECITAL.

Fig. 4. Literary and Philosophical Society's Lectures, 1893 (Eastern Morning News)

So deep was the apathy to secondary education that even the Grammar School had a constant struggle to obtain and keep pupils.[9]

Even in 1895 with a population of over 200 000 not many more than 500 boys and girls were receiving a secondary education. The educational standard of many adults was consequently quite low

Led by Dr Kelburne King, a surgeon interested in science and education, and Albert Rollit, a solicitor and Alderman, the Royal Institution became one of the main centres for adult education in Hull after 1872. Science classes that qualified for the Science and Art Department's grants were held. Saturday afternoon lectures took place in its museum and the Literary and Philosophical Society's lectures greatly improved. The university extension movement was introduced from Cambridge in 1876, two lecture courses took place in 1876-7 and the first three year course commenced the following year. Rollit had visions of the Royal Institution gaining university status and in 1878 suggested that a college be formed. A committee was set-up in 1880 but the following year only £424 had been subscribed and the scheme had to be abandoned. However the Institution continued to develop and after 1883 it had a chemistry laboratory in Bond Street with a permanent salaried lecturer, G. Carr Robinson. The Hull School of Art had opened in 1861 with grants from the Science and Art Department to teach applied art and industrial design for local manufacturers; both day and evening classes were held. The School became affiliated with the Royal Institution after 1875 and moved to 2 Albion Street.

Following the failure to set up a university college in Hull an attempt was made to establish a technical school, principally advocated by T. B. Holmes, a local businessman, and Francis Bond, Principal of Hull and East Riding College after 1881. In 1887 a Mayor's Queen's Jubilee Fund opened to provide a technical school, however, this only attracted promises of £292. By 1904 only £50 had been paid and the money was invested in Hull Corporation stocks with the income going for prizes at the then established Technical School.

BRITAIN'S INFERIORITY

A surprising boost to technical education came with the Great Exhibition of 1851. Designed to show Great Britain's industrial superiority, it only revealed a falling behind compared to Continental Europe, as shown by the Report of the Commissioners of the Great Exhibition. *"We have confessed likewise that ... this is the only country that has neither supplied ... scientific or artistic instruction to its industrial population; nor, for men of science and art, a centre of action, and of exchange of the result of their labours ... Yet this country, as the centre of commerce and industry of the world, would seem to require, more than any other, to have these wants supplied; and the Great Exhibition has, in its results convinced us that unless they be speedily procured, this country will run serious risk of losing that pre-eminent position which now makes its strength and its boast."*[10]

As a result the Science and Art Department, in Sou Kensington, part of the Board of Trade, came into existence in 1853. It did much to guide and encourage teaching of science subjects, but was less successful in co-ordinating the content of its classes with the needs of industry. The Department took advice from employers and decided that there was no place for Government sponsored workshop training only theoretical teaching. The Science and Art Department moved to the newly formed Board of Education in 1856 and provided grants from 1859 based on examination results. Payment by result actually led to a reduction in the number of science classes as fewer pupils passed science exams. Lack of teacher training led to some shoddy practice; it has been asserted that some candidates were able to pass the examination in chemistry without having had any practical experience in a laboratory. However, science now had a permanent place in the school curriculum.

The Paris Exhibition of 1867 reinforced Great Britain's technological inferiority. Sir Lyon Playfair, who had been trying to "educate the nation" since the 1850s, returned from the Exhibition and commented that *"the one cause of this inferiority upon which there was most unanimity is that France, Prussia, Austria, Belgium and Switzerland possess good systems of industrial education for the masters and managers of factories and workshops and that England possesses none"*.[11] Playfair had helped to organise the 1851 Exhibition.

The perception that something had to be done about technical education resulted in the Royal Commission of Scientific Instruction and the Advancement of Science, under the chairmanship of the seventh Duke of Devonshire, in 1872-5. This confirmed that Great Britain was falling behind foreign competition and pointed out that the government was prepared to support geological sciences, whereas sciences that contributed most to economic progress were neglected.

Stimulated by the Devonshire Commission a meeting of the London Livery Companies in 1876 instigated the City and Guilds of London Institute for the Advancement of Technical Education. Its aims were *"to provide and encourage education adapted to the requirements of all classes of persons engaged, or preparing to engage, in manufacturing or other industries"*.[12] Part time classes were held for workers, but the students who attended even the most elementary of City and Guild technical classes were, in many cases, insufficiently prepared to profit by teaching. An improvement in elementary education would have resulted from compulsory state attendance; however, Church bodies were eager to preserve their dominant position in education and manufactures and landowners also opposed compulsory school attendance.

The City & Guilds founded the Finsbury Technical College in 1883. It was designed as a *"model trade school for the instruction of artisans and other persons preparing for intermediate posts in industrial works"*.[13] It taught mechanical and offered electrical engineering, technical subjects, chemistry, applied arts and held trade classes. This became the pattern for technical colleges elsewhere.

A further Royal Commission on Technical Instruction, under Sir Bernard Samuelson, reported in 1884. It concluded that *"our industrial empire is vigorously attacked all over the world. We find that our most formidable assailants are the best educated peoples"*.[14] The Report recommended that local authorities be empowered, if they think fit, to contribute to the establishment and maintenance of secondary and technical schools or colleges. A witness before the select committee stated that *"I do not know a single manager of ironworks in Yorkshire who understands the simple elements of chemistry"*.[15] The report also specifically mentioned Hull's backwardness in the provision of technical education compared to similar cities.

THE CREATION OF TECHNICAL SCHOOLS

The 1888 Local Government Act set up county and county borough councils thereby placing the onus for further organisation and establishment of technical schools on local authorities. The Cross Report, also of 1888, recommended transferring responsibility for technical instruction to the Education Department although only at an elementary level.

The Technical Instruction Act of 1889 gave the new local authorities the power to levy a 1d in the pound rate to supply technical instruction by funding schools, appointing teachers, etc. The Act defined technical instruction as that given *"in the principles of science and art applicable to industries and in the application of special branches of science and art to specific industries and employment's"*.[16] It was expressly stated that the instruction should not include the practice of any trade or industry. This was directly opposite to the Continental view, where the importance of workshop apprenticeship received strong emphasis.

For the first time local authorities could spend money on education other than at an elementary level. A financial accident encouraged local authorities to promote technical education. In 1890 a Government proposal that a tax on spirits should be given to the new county councils, partly for police superannuation and partly for the purchase of publican's licences to reduce the number of public houses, was fought by Sir William Mather, a Manchester Electrical Engineer, and Arthur Acland MP who argued that the proceeds should go to technical education in England and Wales. The Government agreed and 'Whisky Money' went to the new County Councils for assisting technical education or reducing the rates. It is perhaps worth a thought that if the temperance movement had been more successful, and spare revenue not been available, municipal technical education would probably not have developed in the way that it did.

HULL'S RESPONSE

The Lord Mayor of Hull, J. T. Woodhouse, in 1891, commented that *"he did not know any town that had been so apathetic on the subject of higher education than Hull"*.[17] With the increase in school leaving age in 1890 the School Boards needed to revise their low cost, low quality approach. Hull Board set-up three higher grade schools loosely based on practical and scientific lines; these were the Central Higher Grade School in Brunswick Avenue (1891), Craven Street (1893) and the Boulevard (1895). All three had good workshops and laboratories, the upper classes formed an Organised Science School under the auspices of the Science and Art Department.

Hull Corporation set-up a Technical Instruction Committee with J. T. Woodhouse (the Mayor) as chairman, on 10 December 1890, to investigate the present position and future needs of technical education in the city. The committee initially also composed of Dr Malet Lambert (Chairman of the School Board), Francis Bond (President of the Literary and Philosophical Society) and A. E. Seaton (President of Hull Technical Education Council). Soon after, the Committee expanded and consisted of 4 Aldermen, 13 Councillors together with representatives of the Chamber of Commerce, Hull School Board, Literary and Philosophical Society, The Church Institute, Young People's Christian and Literary Institute (YPI), Hull Technical Education Council, Hull Institution of Engineers and Naval Architects, the School of Art, University Extension Society and Trinity House School, three employers and three employees who were representative of local industries and three co-opted members of special experience.

The Committee sent a letter to interested bodies in 1890 inviting suggestions on how the whisky money could be best spent and their responses are given below.

The School Board promoted its new Central Higher Grade School that they had set-up in anticipation of the Technical Instruction Act. It contained the best chemical laboratory in the North and East Ridings (according to the Board), a physical Laboratory, a specially fitted cooking lecture room and 23 class rooms. They thought that most of the available grant should go to them. The Technical Instruction Committee, however, thought that the School Board was ineligible for any grant and should not be paid any even if eligible. The committee disliked the Board's policy of not allowing any of their qualified teachers to lecture in voluntary institutions. Grant aid would partly be spent on heating, rent, etc. from which the Board was already exempt and they still had unspent funds. Also the Board had been the only body able to establish free evening institutes under the rates but they spent the money on Science and Art Department classes instead. Few other Councils were funding School Boards with technical instruction grant and funding the Hull Board would scatter already thin resources. After an appeal to the Science and Art Department the School Board received an allocation of the grant money. The School Board had suspected that the Technical Instruction Committee was biased against them as most of its members were representatives of rival institutes.

The Literary and Philosophical Society mentioned that only they provided advanced instruction through their Chair of Chemistry with its laboratory, lecture theatre and apparatus. Their permanent, salaried chemistry lecturer, Mr G. Carr Robinson, had 10 years experience teaching chemistry and its application to the manufacture of oil, colours and varnishes. For 1891 they had 35 passes from the Science and Art Department in Chemistry and 5 passes from the City and Guilds of

Fig. 5. Church Institute, Albion Street (N.U.T. Conference Souvenir, 1912)

and that lower instruction be left to existing agencies.

The YPI had established adult Science Classes in Hull by 1869. In 1887 they erected 4 specially designed Lecture Rooms at a cost of £1400 for their 1700 to 1800 students, they also had 13 educational rooms and provided 85 different classes, 61 of which were within the definition of technical instruction. In 1891 they had had 99 first class and 297 second class passes from the Science and Art Department and 8 passes from the City and Guilds. They recommended a Technical School for higher stages and that existing classes should continue to be funded.

The Church Institute mentioned that they had been pioneers of technical instruction in Hull and recommended the foundation of a Technical School. Hull and East Riding College also applied for a grant but was ineligible.

Individuals were also consulted, for example, G. Krause PhD recommended a commercial department, Hull being especially connected with continental countries. Many institutions and individuals thought that there should be more provision for women.

London in Oils, Colours and Varnishes. They recommended centralised control of instruction.

T. B. Holmes, President of the Hull University Extension Society, pointed out that they had begun in 1876 and that 100 Terminal Certificates and 55 vice-chancellor certificates had been granted since then. The Society had maintained a Saturday Morning class with an average attendance of 400. They recommended a Collegiate body composed of existing agencies.

The School of Art had 260 to 320 students and already taught industrial and decorative art and might be able to include mechanical and architectural drawing. Hull Technical Education Council recommended a Collegiate body with seven chairs for higher instruction

The Grammar School said that it taught lower middle class boys, many of whose parents could not afford the very moderate and very low fee of £4 4s per annum (a third of most endowed schools). On leaving boys usually found employment in merchants' offices or retail shops and workshops. Mathematics was taught for 17½ hours out of a total of 25 school hours per week, French and German were also taught. For an extra 5s per quarter they could give instruction in drawing, shorthand and typesetting.

Local authorities in other parts of the country had already decided to spend the whole of the Local Taxation Grants on technical education and Hull followed suit. Teaching the lower stages of Science and Art Department classes was left to existing institutions with a number of improvements. Teachers were to be paid fixed salaries, not by results, the number of lessons per week increased and better methods of teaching adopted. Most classes took place in the evening. For higher level technical instruction lectures were taken by staff of secondary schools and the University Extension Society. The East Riding County Council and the County Borough of Hull had expected to receive £7306 from the grants, however, in 1891 Hull only received £2853 (the total income of the Hull

Council in 1891 was £16,607 7s 4d). Local institutions received £850 for instruction given in 1890. The allocation of grant aid for 1890 was as follows:

Institution	Grant(£)
YPI	225
Hull University Extension Society	112 10s
Church Institute	100
Lit. & Phil. Society	112 10s
School of Art	75
Grammar School	75
School Board	150

Funding for 1891 was similar except the School Board received £200 and the following year it received £300. From the Exchequer the Committee received £3144 10s in 1892, £3029 5s 4d in 1893 and £3032 11s 11d in 1894.

THE MUNICIPAL TECHNICAL SCHOOL

Funding rival organisations proved unworkable and in December 1892 the Technical Instruction Committee decided to found and maintain Hull Corporation Technical Schools. They were aware of the drawbacks *"but we are of opinion that by combining the business capacity in the Technical Committee with the special experience for which drafts may be made outside its ranks, such a governing body*

may be constituted as may be fitted to grapple success with this important and complicated educational problem and to be able to win and retain the confidence of the town."[18] The Council gave its approval in May 1893. The plan envisaged five schools each administered by its own subcommittee of the Technical Instruction Committee, namely: Department of Engineering and Cognate Industries, Mercantile and Commercial Department, Department for Technical Instruction of Women, Technology Department and a Department of Higher Instruction in Science. For each department the Committee suggested a range of appropriate courses and the level of grant.

"Department of Engineering and Cognate Industries

Mechanical Engineering with Naval Architecture and Shipbuilding. Civil Engineering with Architecture, Surveying, Building Construction. Carpentry and Joinery. Shipwright's work, Ship-Joinery, Brickwork and Masonry. This group of industries was seen as the most important in Hull that could benefit from technical instruction. Maintained with a grant of £600. It was felt desirable that a separate building with a mechanics workshop, tools and appliances for practical work should be built.

Mercantile and Commercial Department

Foreign Languages; German, French, Spanish and Scandinavian. Commercial Arithmetic. Commercial Geography. Shorthand. Typewriting.
Hull is much more of a distributing than a manufacturing centre, and therefore special attention should be given to instruction in mercantile and commercial subjects. No expensive buildings or apparatus would be required therefore it needed a grant of only £270. Rooms in Board Schools could be used for evening classes.

Department of Technical Instruction of Women

Departments to include; cookery, laundry, nursing, sewing, dressmaking, knitting and domestic economy. Maintained with a grant of £100. Rooms in Board Schools could be used for evening classes.

Technical Department

Departments to include: coaltar products, oils, varnishes and colours, gas manufacture, iron and steel, leather tanning and dressing of skins, photography, telegraphy and telephony, electric lighting, plumbers work, typography, lithography and milling. Because the
Technical Instruction Act did not allow teaching the practice of any trade it would be necessary to obtain consent of the Science and Art Department for permission to give instruction. Rooms in Board Schools could be used for evening classes.

Department of Higher Scientific Instruction

Very few classes had been held in higher stages of scientific instruction mainly due to the high cost of apparatus and staff. The Committee proposed two departments of chemistry and its applications and physical sciences (to include sound, light, heat, magnetism and electricity). Chemistry funded with £300 grant and physical sciences received £450. The laboratories of the Literary and Philosophical Society and the Higher Grade School could be used for chemistry classes. The Committee thought that the grant to the physical sciences department would be better spent on a lecturer with a science degree and apparatus rather than a new building. Science lectures could be held in the lecture halls of the Literary and Philosophical Society, YPI and the Higher Grade Board School."

Fees charged were to be low and remitted if a student was thought meritorious, scholarships were given to working men to enable them to obtain higher technical instruction. Initially the Committee wanted to give free places to some or all of its students, however the Science and Art Department ruled that they could only give scholarships to poor students if they passed an entrance examination.

After 1892 all grants to other institutions providing technical instruction were discontinued, the whole of the funds going to directly supplying technical and manual instruction. Four subcommittees of the Technical Instruction Committee administered the different departments, i.e. Engineering and Cognate Industries, Commercial and Mercantile, Women's Department and the Finance and General Purposes Subcommittee.

The Committee wanted to appoint a Principal to act as Organising Officer and Educational Adviser similar to other University Colleges specialising in technical courses. "*A well managed college, under a competent Principal, will earn large sums, not only in the shape of students' fees, but in Government Grants, and the salary attached to the office should easily be recouped.*"[19] To appoint an Organising Secretary on a small salary and replacing him with a Principal later on was seen by the Committee as false economy, a Principal should be paid around £500 according to a report by London County Council this was accepted by the Committee but reduced a few months later to £350. It was not possible to make an appointment until 1894.

G. Carr Robinson, teacher of chemistry at the Literary and Philosophical Society, was appointed Professor of Chemistry on 28 August 1893 at a salary of £150 per annum, thus becoming the first member of staff at the new college. Robinson was formerly Demonstrator of chemistry in the University of Edinburgh. Part time teachers for the evening classes were also appointed: E. Quibell (brickwork and masonry), J. W. Smith (carpentry and joinery), A. N. Somerscales and H. Evington (mechanical engineering), J. W. Abram (flour milling) and C. H. Kitching and T. H. Brown (plumbing). They all received a salary of £14 for 28 lectures. Dr. J. Wright Mason was appointed to run Preventative Medicine and Sanitary Science. Classes were announced in the local newspapers and by posters in the town.

All the technical department classes were held at the YPI, except practical plumbing that took place in Mr Harrison's workshops at 30 George Street. The room was rented at £12 a year. Student fees were set at 2s 6d except theoretical chemistry and plumbing, which were 5s.

THE FIRST CLASSES

In October 1893 the Hull Municipal Technical School (the name changed to Hull Municipal Technical College in 1909) started its first classes bringing, for the first time, systematic technical education to Hull. For the opening session there were 176 students paying a total of £31/7/6 in fees.

Subject	No. of Students
Chemistry, theoretical	31
Chemistry, practical	32
Carpentry & Joinery	13
Milling (flour)	16
Brickwork & Masonry	7
Mechanical Engineering	5
Plumbing, theoretical & practical	5 operatives
Do.	34 apprentices
Plumbing, theoretical	2 apprentices
Sanitary Science	31

A student who took the City and Guilds Ordinary Grade examination in Milling obtained the first prize of £2 offered by the Pewterer's Company, and was awarded the Silver Medal given by the City and Guilds of London Institute. The Committee thought the chemistry results from examinations held by

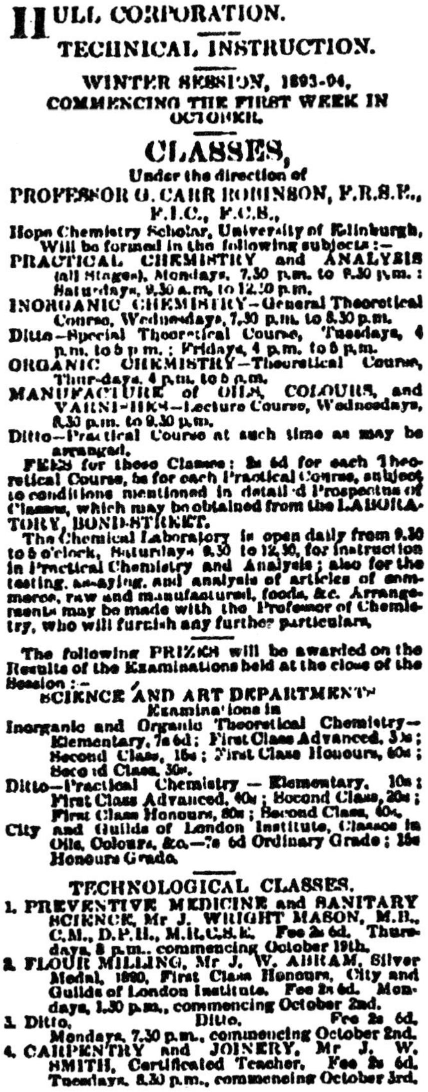

HULL CORPORATION.

TECHNICAL INSTRUCTION.

WINTER SESSION, 1893-94,
COMMENCING THE FIRST WEEK IN OCTOBER.

CLASSES,
Under the direction of
PROFESSOR G. CARR ROBINSON, F.R.S.E., F.I.C., F.C.S.,
Hope Chemistry Scholar, University of Edinburgh,
Will be formed in the following subjects:—

PRACTICAL CHEMISTRY and ANALYSIS (all Stages), Mondays, 7.30 p.m. to 9.30 p.m.; Saturdays, 9.30 a.m. to 12.30 p.m.
INORGANIC CHEMISTRY—General Theoretical Course, Wednesdays, 7.30 p.m. to 8.30 p.m.
Ditto—Special Theoretical Course, Tuesdays, 4 p.m. to 5 p.m.; Fridays, 4 p.m. to 5 p.m.
ORGANIC CHEMISTRY—Theoretical Course, Thursdays, 4 p.m. to 5 p.m.
MANUFACTURE of OILS, COLOURS, and VARNISHES—Lecture Course, Wednesdays, 8.30 p.m. to 9.30 p.m.
Ditto—Practical Course at such time as may be arranged.

FEES for these Classes: 2s 6d for each Theoretical Course, 5s for each Practical Course, subject to conditions mentioned in detailed Prospectus of Classes, which may be obtained from the LABORATORY, BOND-STREET.

The Chemical Laboratory is open daily from 9.30 to 5 o'clock, Saturdays 9.30 to 12.30, for instruction in Practical Chemistry and Analysis; also for the testing, assaying, and analysis of articles of commerce, raw and manufactured, foods, &c. Arrangements may be made with the Professor of Chemistry, who will furnish any further particulars.

The following PRIZES will be awarded on the Results of the Examinations held at the close of the Session:—

SCIENCE AND ART DEPARTMENT
Examinations in
Inorganic and Organic Theoretical Chemistry—Elementary, 7s 6d; First Class Advanced, 3[illegible]s; Second Class, 15s; First Class Honours, 60s; Second Class, 30s.
Ditto—Practical Chemistry — Elementary, 10s; First Class Advanced, 40s; Second Class, 20s; First Class Honours, 80s; Second Class, 60s.
City and Guilds of London Institute, Classes in Oils, Colours, &c.—7s 6d Ordinary Grade; 15s Honours Grade.

TECHNOLOGICAL CLASSES.
1. PREVENTIVE MEDICINE and SANITARY SCIENCE, Mr J. WRIGHT MASON, M.B., C.M., D.P.H., M.R.C.S.E. Fee 2s 6d. Thursdays, 8 p.m., commencing October 19th.
2. FLOUR MILLING, Mr J. W. ABRAM, Silver Medal, 1890, First Class Honours, City and Guilds of London Institute. Fee 2s 6d. Mondays, 1.30 p.m., commencing October 2nd.
3. Ditto, Ditto. Fee 2s 6d. Mondays, 7.30 p.m., commencing October 2nd.
4. CARPENTRY and JOINERY, Mr J. W. SMITH, Certificated Teacher. Fee 2s 6d. Tuesdays, 8.30 p.m., commencing October 3rd.

Fig. 6. Advert for the first classes at the Technical School, September 1893. (Eastern Morning News)

HULL YOUNG PEOPLE'S CHRISTIAN AND LITERARY INSTITUTE, CHARLOTTE-STREET.

SESSION 1893-4.

THE SCIENCE, ART, AND GENERAL CLASSES

Commence in the Week beginning SEPTEMBER 25TH.

The PROSPECTUS of 100 CLASSES

IN

SCIENCE and ART, and in PRACTICAL, COMMERCIAL, MUSICAL, and GENERAL SUBJECTS,

Together with Full Particulars of

EVERY DEPARTMENT OF THE INSTITUTE

may be obtained of the Librarian,

At the INSTITUTE, CHARLOTTE-STREET.

Fig. 7. YPI Classes, 1893 (Hull Daily Mail)

the Science and Art Department in Theoretical and Practical Chemistry were disappointing and appointed two assistants for the lecture room and laboratory. Two students had been successful in passing the Theoretical and Practical Registration Examinations held by the Worshipful Company of Plumbers.

Dr. J. Riley DSc became the Technical School's first Director of Studies and Organising Secretary in March 1894, at the age of 35, 142 applicants had applied for the post. John Thomas Riley had previously been a teacher at Stockport elementary school from 1873-77. Demonstrator and assistant lecturer in experimental physics at Mason College, Birmingham, 1880-83 and Second Master of Bradford Technical College from 1883. He obtained a Degree of Doctor of Science in 1886, his subject for the Doctorate being 'Electricity treated Mathematically'. Both Mason College and Bradford Technical College had only just been established when Riley was appointed, he gained much practical experience setting-up and developing new departments and classes.

Dr Riley asked for an increase in his salary in 1896 as he effectively held three posts, Principal and General Organiser (Riley disliked the term Director of Studies and preferred to call himself Principal), Head of the Department of Mathematics and Pure and Applied Physics and General Secretary. He revealed that only two months after his appointment he had been offered the post of Principal and Head of a department at another Technical School for £400. The Committee agreed to increase his salary to £400.

Dr. Riley was asked to produce a report on the Committee's Scheme for providing Technical Instruction, this he completed within a month of his appointment. In his report Riley recommended *"a full time Senior Department for advanced mechanical, electrical and civil engineering; a two year full time Junior Technical School for the preparatory training of those of lower attainments, grouped courses in all branches of building, plumbing and sanitation, and engineering; a full time three year course in commerce and modern languages; a long list of evening subjects including printing, fisheries, women's work and the absorption of the School of Art"*. Most of these recommendations were in place when the first prospectus appeared in September 1894, although accommodation remained a serious problem for the 55 full time students and 645 evening students. The full time students included 27 junior technicals, 12 junior commercials, 4 senior engineers, 7 senior chemists and 5 physicists.

The range of evening classes was quite wide including 44 students in engineering, 10 in electrical engineering, 19 telegraphy and telephony, 35 pure and applied chemistry, 68 mathematics and physics, 33 carpentry and joinery, 8 brickwork, 64 plumbing and sanitary science, 13 naval architecture, 20 flour milling and 122 in women's industries, chiefly dressmaking, cookery and laundry work. On the commercial side there were 152 students study-

Fig. 8. Dr. John Thomas Riley. (N.U.T. Conference Souvenir, 1912)

ing mainly shorthand, bookkeeping and English with 39 studying French, 14 German and 4 Scandinavian. Attendances fluctuated throughout the year.

More full time staff were employed in September 1894. Richard Durley

as Chief Lecturer on Engineering with a salary of £250 a year. He trained in the engineering department of University College, Bristol and in the engineering department of University College, London; graduated as BSc in mathematics and physics; served apprenticeship

HULL

Municipal

𝕿𝖊𝖈𝖍𝖓𝖎𝖈𝖆𝖑 𝕾𝖈𝖍𝖔𝖔𝖑.

PROSPECTUS.

SESSION 1894-5.

Fig. 9. Frontispiece from the first prospectus (HC)

with Earle's Company where he was a draughtsman and lecturer to the Company's engineering pupils. John Firth became Assistant Master for Mathematics and Drawing at a salary of £120 per annum after

the Committee's first choice was unable to accept the offer. John Menzies, Jun. as Teacher of Drawing. Thomas Spence as Instructor in Woodwork at a salary of £100; he was a joiner by trade and had acted

as Joiner Instructor for the Prison Commissioners of Scotland for three years and had experience erecting large buildings. Thomas Gorton as Instructor in Metalworking at a salary of £100, he had been Mechanic in the engineering department of Mason College, Birmingham. Reginald Proudlove and Robert Hutchinson were appointed Assistant Lecturers in Physics and Mathematics each at a salary of £120 per annum.

For some of the Commercial Department appointments the age range was limited to between 25 and 40. Mons O Baumann became French and German Master at a salary of £200 per annum. Thomas Jackson was the English Master at £150 a year. In the Women's Industries Department Violet Freeborough was appointed Teacher of Cookery and Laundry Work. She held a Diploma from the National Training School of Cookery in 1892, she had previously kept a school and lectured at the Hull Church Institute. Mrs Overton was appointed Teacher of Dressmaking for a course of twelve lessons at 10s per evening and Miss H. Hauge became Teacher of Millinery at 8s for each two hour lesson.

T. G. Baker became Teacher of Naval Architecture and Ship Carpentry at 7s 6d per hour and J. W.

Smith was appointed Teacher of Building Construction, Carpentry and Joinery with two, two hour, building construction classes per week at £21 per session and 7s 6d per hour for carpentry and joinery. C. J. Gill was appointed Teacher of Ship Joinery at 7s 6d per hour. W. H. Hamer, of the North Eastern Railway Co., became an evening lecturer in Brickwork and Masonry at 7s 6d per hour and Mr Scotter, of Earle's Shipbuilding Co., took Pattern Making classes at 6s per evening. Mr Raylor, Mr Rank's foreman, was appointed Teacher of Milling at £14 per session there were two, one hour, classes per week, he replaced Mr Abram. The plumbing classes were very popular and T. H. Brown had to be appointed Assistant Teacher of Plumbing for the Wednesday and Friday evening classes at 5s 6d per night.

NEW PREMISES

After the first year the Technical School still only had the Chemical Laboratory in Bond Street that they could call their own premises with most of the other subjects being taught in rooms rented from the YPI or in Board Schools. The Technical Instruction Committee also needed to appoint a relatively large number of lecturers, trying primarily to recruit them from industry.

The Engineering School was established in a former brewery at 86 Osborne Street owned by Edward Robson and was provided with workshops at a cost of £1650 in 1894, it was hoped that these would only be temporary premises. Teachers in the new school were apparently annoyed by boys looking in at the windows and blinds had to be installed. A science lecture room and a physical laboratory at the Gymnasium, Osborne Street might also have been used (Science and Technology Department). Women's Industries and the General Office occupied the ground floor of 7 Albion Street with the Commercial Department on the first floor. The Albion Street premises had been the High School for Girls owned by the Church Day School Company, the Committee rented it, exclusive of the stables, for £85 a year from 1894. Free classes for fishermen were provided at St. Andrews Hall, St. Andrews Dock, from 1895 under the tuition of Reuben Manton. The Chemistry Department used the Laboratory in Bond Street and plumbing workshops were rented from Harrison's at Crown Buildings, George Street.

EXPANSION PLANS

In April 1893 a plan was proposed by the Public Libraries Committee to build a 'central hall' combining a central library, public hall and technical college. The Municipal Technical School would have four schools of chemistry, physics, engineering and women's industries with workshops for manual instruction and rooms for technical instruction, such as plumbing and cooking, classrooms for teaching mercantile and other subjects, music room, a school of art, art galleries and an educational museum. Five sites were suggested: Prospect Street, Baker Street, Paragon Street, Kingston Square and Corporation Field in Park Street. By the end of 1895 the Public Libraries and Technical Instruction Committees had chosen Corporation Field. However the Property Committee rejected the plan stating that *"This Committee (recognising the value of the Corporation Field as an open space for the immediate neighbourhood, and also its importance as a Central Market) cannot see their way to recommend the Council to accede to the application of the Public Libraries and Technical Instruction Committees."*[20] No alternative sites were suggested so the scheme did not develop and the technical

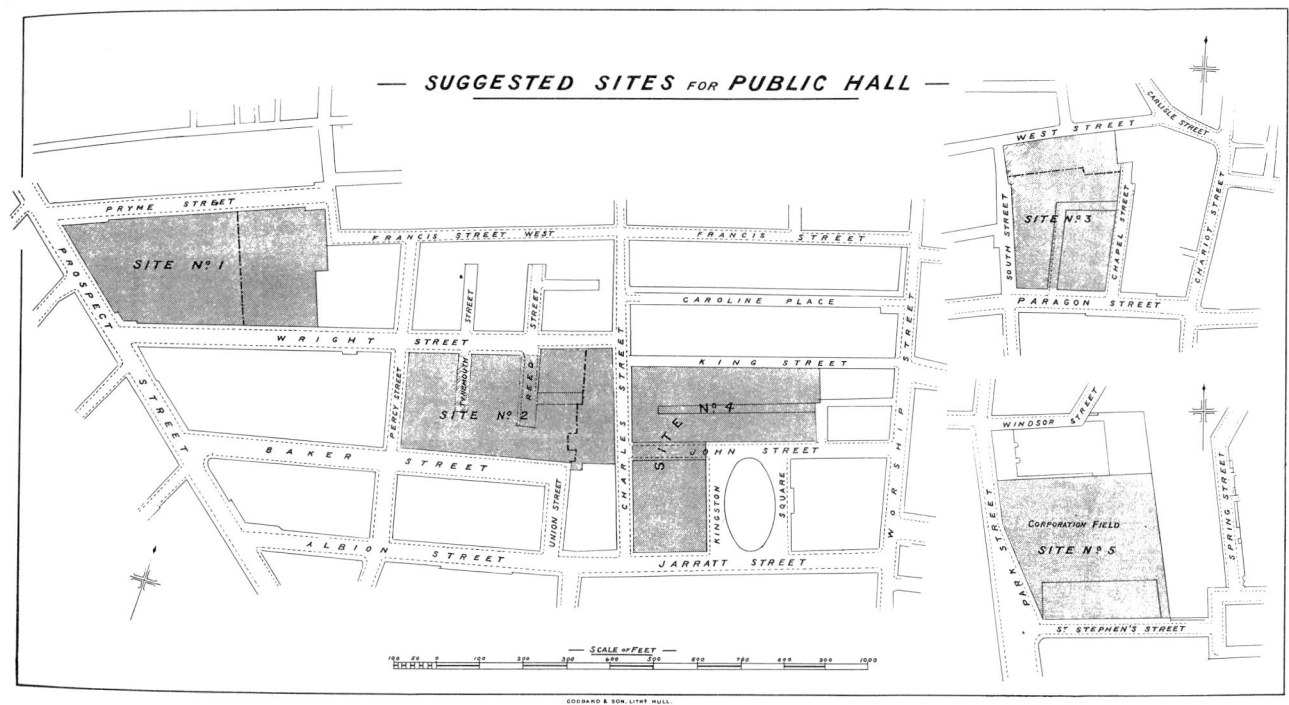

Fig. 10. Plans of alternative sites for the new 'Central Hall' 1893 (HC)

school remained in its cramped rooms.

Hull Municipal Technical School officially opened on 14 January 1895 with a ceremony at the Osborne Street premises. The visitors were taken on a tour of the Physical Laboratory by Dr Riley who pointed out that equal time was given to theoretical and practical work. Mr Durley showed them the machine shop and the Drawing Department where the opening then took place. The Mayor expressed the hope that the premises were only temporary and acknowledged the work of the Royal Institution and the YPI over the last twenty years. Mr Laverack, Chairman of the Technical Instruction Committee, also regretted that the present buildings were not permanent. The Mayor had been struck by a statement by Professor Huxley made at the Inauguration of the Imperial Institute in 1887 and quoted "*I do not think I am far wrong in assuming that we are entering - indeed, have already entered - upon the most serious struggle for existence to which this country has ever been committed. The latter years of the century promise to see us embarked in an industrial war of far more serious import than the military wars of earlier years.*"[21] C. H. Wilson MP mentioned that one of his firm's agents abroad had said that England was not getting on commercially as well as she should do and that England was positively going down the hill rather than up. Perhaps rather complacently he added *"well, at present we were on a considerable eminence, and could possibly afford to slide a small way without being much the worse for it"*.[22] Mr J. Stuart JP stated that he was glad that at last the residents of Hull could compete with Manchester, Bradford and Liverpool where technical instruction had been taught for many years.

PARK STREET

The engineering laboratory had been set-up but in too small an area and the work had to be split among three rooms making supervision difficult. The atmosphere in the Osborne Street premises was quite literally poisonous due to poor ventilation that could only partly be relieved. Vibration from the physical laboratory was a real problem making some necessary experiments impossible and the chemistry laboratory was very over crowded. The Inspector from the Science and Art Department commented that *"the Laboratory is very well supplied with necessary appliances for Elementary and Advanced work, though accommodation seems scarcely up to the needs of the Technical School"*.[23] The accommodation in the Commercial School was also inadequate

Fig. 11. Apprentice pieces probably in the Osborne Street premises (HC)

and they had to rent rooms in the Sculcoates Parochial Hall, bringing the total number of buildings wholly or partly occupied by the School to seven.

A partial solution to the lack of permanent buildings occurred when the Sailors' Orphan Homes moved to new premises on Cottingham Road in 1898. They offered their old building in Park Street to the Technical Instruction Committee for £6500 in February 1897. Alterations, equipment and furniture cost a further £8500 before the college could fully move in at the end of July 1898. The Park Street site contained 5251 sq. yds. and it was thought that the Technical School would only need 2500 - 3000 so there would be plenty of room for expansion. John Bilson was appointed as architect for the alterations. His original plans would have cost £12000 including moving the Art School to Park Street. However, the Art School was against the move. *"In view of the proximity of the present School of Art to the Museum and proposed Art Gallery, which are to be taken over by the Technical Instruction Committee, and of the advantage derived therefrom by the students of the School, this Committee is of the view that*

Fig. 12. The schoolroom, Sailor's Orphan Homes, Park Street (Adventures in Sympathy, 1935)

It is very satisfactory to note that the School is steadily growing in usefulness and public appreciation as is shown by the increasing number of students enrolling in the evening classes."[25]

The former dormitory at the front of the Orphan's Homes became the commercial department and the old schoolhouse at the rear accommodated the engineering block. A new corridor connecting the two buildings housed the chemistry, physics, woodwork and engineering drawing departments. Despite the alterations conditions inside Park Street were still inadequate for the increasing number of students.

The leases on the Osborne Street and Albion Street premises were given up at the end of July 1898, although Osborne Street still seems to have been used by the Technical School in the early 1900s.

the Art School should not be removed to the new premises in Park Street."[24] Bilson's revised plans were estimated to cost £7600. Mark Harper won the contract to carry out the alterations for £8193 and work began on 22 February 1898. How to heat the building seems to have occupied much of the time of the Committee, eventually they decided that 78 radiators would be needed, although these were probably inadequate judging by the number of complaints over the years. The Science and Art Department Inspectors were pleased with the Technical School and looked forward to the move. *"As a result of my three visits to this School (86 Osborne Street), I have satisfied myself of the general efficiency of the teaching and satisfactory organisation of the work. In a school of this kind practical work by the students is a main feature of the institution, and for this the laboratories and workshops give satisfactory accommodation, which will be much improved when the classes are transferred to the newly acquired premises in Park Street.*

Notes for Chapter One

1.   G. Roderick & M. Stevens, The British Malaise, Falmer Press, 1982.

2.   H. Barnard, A Short History of English Education from 1760-1944, L.U.P., 1958.

3.   K. Allison, The Victoria County History of the Counties of England, A History of the County of York East Riding, Vol. 1, O.U.P., 1969.

4.   Manchester Statistical Society, Report into the State of Education in Hull, 1841.

5.   Ibid.

6.   H. Barnard, A Short History of English Education, 1958.

7.   K. Allison, V.C.H., Vol. 1, O.U.P., 1969.

8.   Ibid.

9.   J. Lawson, Middle Class Education,

10.   Second Report of the Commissioners of the Great Exhibition, 1841.

11.   J. Lang, City & Guilds of London Institute 1878-1978, City & Guilds of London Institute, 1978.

12.   D. Bratchell, The Aims and Organisation of Further Education, Pergamon press, 1968.

13.   H. Barnard, A Short History of English Education, L.U.P., 1958.

14.   J. Lawson & H. silver, A Social History of Education in England, Methuen, 1973.

15.   M. Argyles, South Kensington to Robbins, Longmans, 1964.

16.   Technical Instruction Act, 1889.

17.   Hull News, 3 October 1891.

18.   Minutes of the Hull Technical Instruction Committee, 19 December 1892.

19.   Ibid., 8 August 1893.

20.   Ibid., 23 July 1896.

21.   Ibid., 30 October 1896.

22.   Ibid.

23.   Ibid.

24.   Ibid., 12 January 1898.

25.   Ibid., 12 May 1898.

NEW RESPONSIBILITIES FOR HULL COUNCIL

The 1902 Education Act replaced 'whisky money' and the penny on the rates and Science and Art Department grants as a source of funding for technical education. It had become difficult to decide who funded which service but the Act cleared this up by making counties and county boroughs (such as Hull City Council) education authorities.

The new Local Education Authorities (LEA's) took over control of evening continuation schools and all elementary and secondary education below university level, in consultation with the Board of Education, that had been organised by the School Board, Technical School or private bodies. After 1926 the evening continuation schools became Evening Institutes classified into Junior and Senior Institutes; Junior Institutes admitted pupils between fourteen and sixteen and the Senior Institutes took adult students.

The new education authorities were not, like the School Boards, ad hoc bodies, directly elected for the sole purpose of administering education. They were elected for all the purposes of local government; but by the Act they were obliged to appoint an education committee to which non-elected people with educational knowledge could be co-opted.

The Act also gave local authorities the power, but not the compulsion, to develop *"technical education in response to the demands made for it by the industries of the country and in close cooperation with them"*.[1]

Fig. 13. Thomas Luxton (HC)

From 30 September 1903 the new Hull Education Committee took over the Technical School with its junior department and evening schools and the School of Art. Initially the Town Clerk was to be the first Secretary or Director of Education with Mr O'Donogue, Clerk of Hull School Board, as Director of Elementary Education and Dr Riley as Director of Higher Education. But O'Donogue did not think the salary sufficient and Riley was appointed Secretary of Education for Hull from 30 September on £650. In 1914 Riley's salary was increased by £100 and his title changed to Director of Education. Mr Luxton, the chemistry teacher, replaced Riley as Superintendent of the Technical School although Riley was still in charge of the Branch School (YPI). The personalities of Riley and Luxton were apparently completely different; Dr Riley was cool, unruffled, far seeing and reserved whilst Mr Luxton was humorous, breezy, wide ranging and talkative with a capacity for organisation and attention to detail. Luxton eventually became Principal in 1906 on a salary of £400.

From the School Board the new Committee took over six evening continuation schools, Charterhouse Lane, Constable Street, Fountain Road, Lime Street, Thomas Barton Holmes and Williamson Street, with a total of 135 pupils. There were additional technical and commercial classes at Central, Boulevard, Craven Street and Daltry Street schools and evening classes in Domestic Studies for Girls at four schools. The attendance at the evening schools had been declining and the Committee decided to bring them into 'organic connection' with the classes at the Technical and Art Schools for which they were considered as preparatory.

The Committee was slow to rise to its new responsibilities and sometimes did so only after remonstrations from the Board of Education. The Board of Education recommended that the Technical School should have more staff, more advanced courses, more co-operation with local industry and that the Junior Technical School and the School of Commerce should be completely detached from the main Technical School. Despite numerous attempts at separation the School of Commerce only became independently administered from 1930 and the Junior School (later Riley High School) from 1947.

THE BEGINNINGS OF A UNIVERSITY

Lord Ripon had proposed the establishment of the Victoria University of Yorkshire to which Hull Technical School could to be affiliated. However in 1904 the University College of Sheffield objected to the word Yorkshire because it implied that the Leeds based Yorkshire College would become the only college in Yorkshire. The House of Lords agreed that there should not be a single non-federal university for the county and refused to grant a Charter.

It had always been the aim of the Hull Corporation to build a comprehensive system of further education based on the Technical School. A plan to combine the School with a new teacher training college emerged in 1906, proposed by a local barrister, W. H. Owen. *"I suggest that the Technical School be shifted to a new site and combined with a day training college for teachers, and that the conjoint institutions be named 'The University College', and a*

Fig. 14. Sports Day, Seniors (HC)

additional accommodation for technical instruction at the present moment. If there should in the future be need for further provision of day technical work, the Board think that the site under discussion would be suitable for the purpose, though the situation would render it unsuitable for further development of evening technical work."[3]

The Hull Education Committee had to agree with the Board of Education but still hoped that other plans in the future might be better supported. After 31 July 1909 grants became available for Teacher Training Colleges and this undoubtedly affected the decision of the Committee to establish a Training College only, rather than a combined college. An area of about 50 acres was bought on Cottingham Road in order *"to provide sites for the Training College and for such extensions and developments of existing institutions as may be deemed desirable at a future time".*[4] The 50 acres divided into about 15 for the training college, 28 for playing fields with a further 6.44 acres fronting Inglemire Lane bought mainly by T. R. Ferens. The Municipal Training College opened in 1913, eventually

curriculum be arranged to prepare students for the BA and BSc of the London University. I also suggest that the present courses and practical subjects taught in the Technical School should be carried on and still further developed in the new college."[2]

The Hull Education Committee approved of the scheme and Riley produced a very detailed report, based on a site on Cottingham Road, but the Board of Education in London objected to the merger pointing to the differences in the type of staff required and to the different sources of finance. The Board's reply was ambiguous as it also said that *"The Board, however, recognise that it is likely that future provision for technical or other higher education will in the course of time be needed in Hull, though it does not appear that any need is shown for the provision of*

Fig. 15. Physical Education exercises in the yard at Park Street (HC)

THE COLLEGE TO THE END OF W.W.1.

The demand for university preparation courses continued to increase and led to some problems for the Technical College. The syllabuses for the preparation courses were different to the College's internal classes although much of the ground was common to both leading to some unnecessary duplication of work for the teachers. To qualify for a university course a pupil either had to pass a matriculation exam at secondary school or begin their preparation in a technical school after they were seventeen. The Technical College to a large extent attracted boys to whom an ordinary secondary school was *"distasteful"*[5] and Luxton thought that if a boy had the ability to obtain a university degree he should not be hampered because he did not attend a school of a particular type.

Even though the commercial classes had moved out of Park Street Luxton predicted that the building would be full again in four or five years time and that rebuilding or the removal of the

becoming part of Hull College of Higher Education in 1976.

The playing fields were used by the High School for Girls, Central Secondary School, Grammar and Technical School besides the Training College. From 1905 the Technical School had used a 10 acre site on the corner of Mill Lane, Anlaby Road, for playing fields offering hockey, football and later cricket. The site is now roughly on the corner of North Road. Mr Luxton did not believe in public competition but thought that simple physical exercise should form part of the regular school curriculum. The Technical School gave up its fields on Anlaby Road when the new facilities on Cottingham Rd. became available. A pavilion was erected, by F. Bilton, on the playing fields in 1911. The Old Boys' Association of the Technical College was also granted permission to erect a pavilion on the playing fields in 1924.

Technical College could not be delayed further. He also hinted that the more urgent the problem the more the Committee adopted a *"laissez faire"*[6] attitude. The Technical College site was only a makeshift one at best and compared unfavourably with the buildings and equipment provided for technical education in other large towns. The ideal for Hull, according to Luxton, would be a great central institution providing for all advanced evening work of every description - a university in character, fed by a well arranged system of preparatory technical, commercial and domestic science schools. He also suggested the Hull could become the central technical school for oils and fats industry for the whole country.

Luxton looked forward to a renaissance in technical education due to lessons learnt early in the First World War. *"The English manufacturer has yet to learn from his German competitor the value of the higher scientific training for the works manager and of the general technical intelligence, apart from a mere single occupation skill, of the worker. The local Technical Colleges must become the Mecca of the manufac-turer, their staffs the honoured confidants of the managers, and their students must be given every opportunity of deserved promotion and every encouragement to advanced work. ... In general, the Technical Colleges must become the intellectual centre for the scientific and technical intelligence of the district, whether in the person of capitalist, works manager, worker or teacher."*[7] He also pointed out that there were no classes in economics in Hull.

POST WAR HOPES AND DIS-APPOINTMENTS

A new technical college was included in the list of building works submitted to Parliament in 1916/17 to be built after the War but events overtook this. The Education Act of 1918, introduced by H. A. L. Fisher, was to have a profound effect on the development of higher education in Hull. The Act envisaged the introduction of compulsory day continuation schools for young people aged 14-16 in employment. This would completely swamp the facilities of the Technical College and the need for reorganisation was obvious. Unfortunately the Act at-tracted much opposition and only Rugby implemented it fully. Hull Education Committee produced its Report on Required Provision for Technical Instruction in May 1918. It commented that *"The commercial, as well as educational policy (in Hull) has been opportunistic, that is, one of waiting till a need has become a necessity before beginning the slow process of providing what is necessary."*[8] If the Act was to be followed the Committee thought the aims of technical colleges in the future would be -

• Advanced teaching to university degree level.
• Consultation work and experimental work - for local industries.
• Investigation and research work - in co-operation with local industries.
• Advanced evening classes.

To satisfy these aims the new Hull Technical College would contain -

• Engineering and ship-building department.
• Department of pure and applied chemistry, including agricultural and

pure and biological science.

Social wing, including a library, gymnasium, dining room, common room, shower baths and possibly an industrial and commercial museum.

A Junior School was to be built nearby but *"so far distant from the college as to obviate the danger of giving the main building the character of too close an association with young boys."*[9]

Correspondents in the local press during November 1918 suggested that a university should be created in Hull as a memorial to those who had lost their lives in the war. One correspondent pointed out that Hull was the largest city without a university and something on the lines of the University of California should be considered. *"Such a school of the truly modern type would attract to itself all the intellectual activity of the district and would be in contact with every aspect of public and industrial life; it would provide for the purely cultural side of education and for the scientific and economic training in which we as a nation are so lamentably deficient."*[10]

An editorial in the Hull Daily Mail also promoted the idea. *"The principle advantage, we repeat, would be to the seniors amongst the youth of the town, who, at present, are not catered for, and who are needed in the fight for commerce which will ensue with rival nations. At present they are crippled and in a way wasted through not being adequately taught. It would enrich the life of the city to have able teachers here, and would make Hull a better and more desirable place to live in, and would speedily justify itself by the results."*[11]

The Head Master of Hymers College thought a university college could develop from the Technical College but that at least £200,000 would be required. Significantly Archdeacon Malet Lambert, Chairman of the Higher Education Sub-Committee, wrote an open letter to the Lord Mayor in the Eastern Morning News. *"There has been a lack of vital continuity between the life of the school and the subsequent practical work of life. Still more has there been a lack of the means for completing the educational equipment we have begun. There has been wanting for the mass of the people the full opportunity to gain higher scientific and technical instruction which a properly equipped institution on an adequate scale alone can give.*

By the wise expenditure of £150,000 we can lay the foundations of an institution which will increase in magnitude and importance as time goes on."[12]

The full Hull Council had approved the scheme by the end of 1918 and they considered *"it essential that without delay an adequate Technical College in preparation for a University ... be erected at an estimated probable cost of £150,000"*.[13] The City Architect began preparing the plans in May 1919.

The Committee recommended that land on Cottingham Road be purchased, by compulsory purchase, next to the training college for the new Technical College. However the purchase had to be deferred as the Acquisition of Land (Assessment of Compensation) Bill was then before Parliament. By the end of July 1920 the Corporation had agreed to buy two fields belonging to Sir Francis Haworth Booth on Cottingham Road and Inglemire Lane. One contained 6.98 acres at £500 per acre and the other contained 8.072 acres at £300 an acre. Two further fields were offered for sale, near the first two fields, in April 1921; they contained 8.416 and 3.36 acres at £500 per acre.

Permission had to be sought from the Board of Education before the 19 acres could be bought for £9378. The Board replied in August 1921 that because of the large amount of money involved it would have to have full details of the new Technical College before they could sanction the sale. By October the Board had reached the decision not to grant permission for the Corporation to buy the land. It justified this by suggesting that the original proposals had been in response to the Education Act of 1918 and that as that Act had not been fully implemented nationally it questioned whether there was any immediate need to expand higher education in Hull. The Board suggested that the present Junior School should be moved to another site, by implication to part of the Cottingham Road land, to allow the senior departments of the College in Park Street to expand if necessary. They also suggested that more evening classes now taken in the College could be moved to

elementary or secondary schools. However, it seems that the real reason for the lack of co-operation from the Board was purely financial; it was prepared to sanction a new Junior School but not an expensive new Technical College. However, by February 1922 the Board even had second thoughts on providing a Junior School and that, *"the increasingly difficult financial conditions obliged them to defer, for the present, their decision upon the Authority's application"*.[14]

In the midst of this gloom T. R. Ferens, chairman of Reckitt & Sons, sent a letter to Francis Askew, Chairman of the Hull Education Committee in March 1922:

"I much regret that the President of the Board of Education has refused his sanction to the purchase

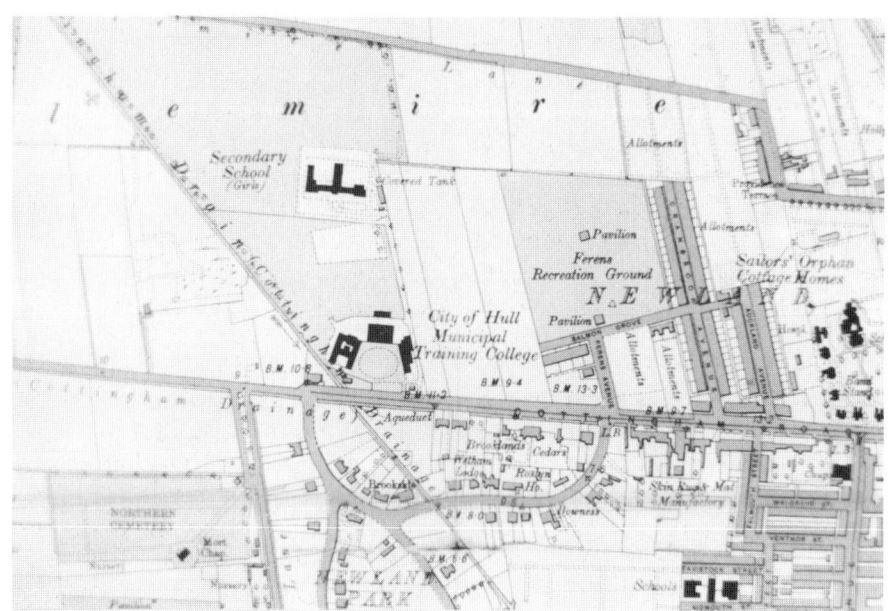

Fig. 16. Site of proposed new Technical College, Cottingham Road, reproduced from the 1919 Ordnance Survey plan.

of the three fields on the Cotting-ham Road, which it was your wish to secure for the purposes of a new Technical College under conditions which would allow of the development of the College into a University.

The site is eminently suitable - it would be a pity to lose it, and it gives me pleasure to say that I shall be glad to buy it and hand it over for the purposes indicated."[15]

Riley again wrote to the Board of Education informing them of the offer. They replied in April 1922, *"I am directed by the Board of Education to express their high appreciation of the offer of the Right Hon. T. R. Ferens, JP, to buy the three fields on the Cotting-ham Road and present them to the Education Committee for the purposes referred to in the Authority's correspondence with the Board. The Board see no reason why this offer should not be accepted".*[16] This completely reversed their original decision of August 1921 although nothing had altered except the financial arrangements. Finally, after three years of trying the new Technical College could be built.

The Corporation completed the purchase of the 19 acres on 2 June 1922 and Ferens handed over a cheque for £9380 5s as payment. The easternmost field was used as elementary school playing fields from 1 September 1923 although the tenant had to be compensated for the loss of his crops. The other two fields remained tenanted and the earliest the Corporation thought they could gain admission was 13 February 1926.

Plans were drawn up for a new Junior Technical School on the Cottingham site in April 1924. Before permission could be granted the Board of Education requested a meeting with Hull Education Committee representatives. After discussions the Board allowed the Junior School to continue as before until the retirement of the Principal.

The Hull Education Committee decided to appoint an Assistant Organiser of Evening Classes in 1925 who would take over the Park Street Evening Technical College when Luxton retired, the Day Technical Institute *"would, no doubt, by then have been transferred to the proposed University College".*[17] A Principal could then be appointed to the new 'Secon-

dary' School (the current Junior School). E. P. Bates was appointed Assistant Organiser in July 1925. However, the Board replying to another request to change recognition from junior to secondary school in August 1926, refused permission as they thought Park Street premises to be unsuitable for a secondary school and that the Junior School would continue to be recognised as before, although they appreciated the unique nature of the school.

If the Hull Corporation had successfully built a Junior School on the Cottingham Road site it would probably have ended any hopes of a university college being established there, although the Corporation did not accept this. It is probably for this reason that Ferens made his very generous offer of £250,000 in Reckitts' shares in November 1925 as the nucleus of a fund for the establishment of a university college. An Organising Committee was quickly set-up consisting of Malet Lambert (Chairman of the Higher Education Sub-Committee), Francis Askew (Chairman of the Education Committee), Dr John Bicker-staff (Clerk to the East Riding County Council), Henry Gore (Headmaster of Hymers College) and Riley; acting in consultation with Luxton and Miss Cumberbirch (Principal of the Hull Municipal Training College).

By the end of 1925 Riley had produced a draft plan for the new college with faculties of Arts, Pure Science, Applied Science, Education and Commerce. After deduction of fees the cost of the existing Senior Departments of Engineering and Chemistry had exceeded £2300 - these departments were to be transferred to the new college. Much of the equipment was over 30 years old and would have to be replaced. Riley estimated that the total cost of the new buildings and equipment would be £150,000 and that the annual amount required for staff and maintenance charges would be around £21,000. The Corporation would be responsible for the erection of the new Technical College and then transfer the site to the Board of the University College.

The next step was to appoint a Principal. Seven candidates were short-listed but it was a very weak field and A. E. Morgan was added to the list by the external assessor. Morgan impressed the Board of the University College but was reluctant to take the post

and would only accept if technology was excluded from the proposed curriculum of the college. Surprisingly his conditions were accepted by the Committee and Morgan was appointed from 18 June 1926. It was quite clear that Morgan, now backed by Ferens, would not allow the Engineering and Chemistry Departments of the Technical College to move to his university college and Riley resigned as Secretary of the University College Board on 16 July 1926. Demoralised at the complete reversal of policy Riley also resigned as Director of Education shortly afterwards and retired to Minehead (as did Mr Luxton). The University College opened in October 1928 with faculties of Arts and Pure Science only but the Technical College had to remain in Park Street.

SOCIAL DEVELOPMENTS AT THE TECHNICAL COLLEGE

The military authorities had been pressing the Technical College to establish a Cadet Corps for several years and in 1921 Luxton decided to poll the parents with quite interesting results. Out of 439 forms sent out only 33 approved of the idea and were willing to bear the expense, 262 parents did not reply. Luxton concluded that the 262 were either indifferent or hostile and abandoned the scheme stating that, *"the position, so far as it has shown itself, is very actively anti-militarist, and that the principals of the League of Nations seems to be more commonly understood than might have been expected"*.[18]

A bronze war memorial was proposed for Park Street in 1923, which can still be seen in the foyer. A room in the Toc. H. building nearby in Londesborough Street was also to be converted into a war memorial in memory of Technical Old Boys who participated in the war. The College also seems to have used rooms in Toc. H. for extra classrooms in the 1960s.

The Technical College held open days for the first time on 10th and 11th of March 1922. It was hoped to attract considerable numbers of the parents of the Day Students on the Friday afternoon and the general public and parents of the evening students at the evening sessions. Luxton estimated that they had three to four thousand members of the public passed through the building on the open days. Some local firms put up exhibitions or held demonstrations.

The Hull Association of Engineers was formed from past and present evening students and staff at the College around 1920. It helped focus public attention and appreciation on the College. There was also an Engineering Consultative Committee and the Plumbing Trades Apprenticeship Advisory Committee established by 1921, these committees provided a link between the College and industry. Luxton hoped that the advisory committees could organise the training of apprentices in most industries on the through-going line of the Kerschensteiner system at Munich. The system of Advisory Committees was developed in 1929/30 to regularise the relation between the Hull Education Committee and the various trades. Advisory Committees were set-up for Retail Trades, Chartered Shipbrokers and Bankers in 1929. By 1932 the number of Advisory Committees had expanded to 12 and the Guild of Building and Field Naturalists Club had been formed at the College. Lecture Room 51 (now F23) at Park Street was modernised during 1934 and used by the affiliated societies for their meetings.

To improve the *"attitude, bearing and behaviour"*[19] of the students the Boys' Council, Students Christian Union and the Historical Guild had been set-up by 1923. The Boys' Council was an elective body, representative of every class in the school, choosing its own chairman and acting independently. The Students Christian Union *"has been a successful attempt to organise the more stable and serious boys of the Senior Departments to set a high standard of personal conduct as an example to all the rest of the school".*[20]

The Historical Guild, which was affiliated to the League of Nations Union, also had a good influence.

The social activities of the College continued to expand and a party of staff and students went on a trip to Paris during the May 1925 holiday. The total number of students in day and evening classes was 6250 taught by a staff of 350. The Junior choir and orchestra attracted 108 men and 92 women.

Some parents had been complaining of the cost of the trams to school. In November 1923 the Tramways Committee introduced a universal penny fare for all secondary students over fourteen.

LUXTON RETIRES

Luxton resigned in December 1925 to take effect from the end of the school year (31 July 1926) and retired to Minehead in 1927. He had moved to Hull in 1895 as assistant master at the Central School; he helped found the Old Boys' Association at the College but was chiefly remembered for establishing the evening institutes. The retirement obviously necessitated some reorganisation; W. S. Cooper, second master of the Junior Day School, was appointed Head Master in independent control of the School (it was hoped that this would be recognised as a secondary school); E. P. Bates became the new Principal of the Technical College and Organiser of all Evening Schools and Classes in Hull. A Board of Studies was formed consisting of Bates, Cooper and the heads of the Engineering and Chemistry Departments chaired by Bates. The Board of Studies lasted until 1929 when the heads of department

Fig. 17. Staff at the Technical College c1924. Luxton is bottom row sixth from left; Walker middle row tenth from left and Bates top row third from left. Sixteen members of staff have been identified. (HC)

were again made directly responsible to the Principal. J. S. Machin became Headmaster of the Central School of Commerce in place of Bates.

On his retirement Luxton wrote. "*I would like to put on record my firm conviction that there is no better work of an educational character done in any type of school than is done in the Technical College, and more especially the part-time classes carried on in them; but progress of these schools is hampered by unsuitable buildings, financial stringency, and a definite hesitation in undertaking new experiments and in extending facilities. I know of no business investment offering such good dividends as the rapid and efficient development of technical education.*"[21]

REGIONAL AND NATIONAL REPORTS

A survey was made by HM Inspectors of further education in Yorkshire for the 1925/26 session, and published in 1927. In 1928 it was considered at a conference of representatives of all the local authorities within the county, together with the representatives of the Universities of Leeds and Sheffield and of Hull University College. From its beginning at this conference the Yorkshire Council for Further Education exercised a profound influence on technical education in Yorkshire, without becoming an examining body. In its main outline and functions it became the prototype for all advisory councils established subsequently throughout the country. It presented the interests of the region in the formation of national policy, and facilitated its working out between neighbouring authorities and their colleges.

Front Elevation

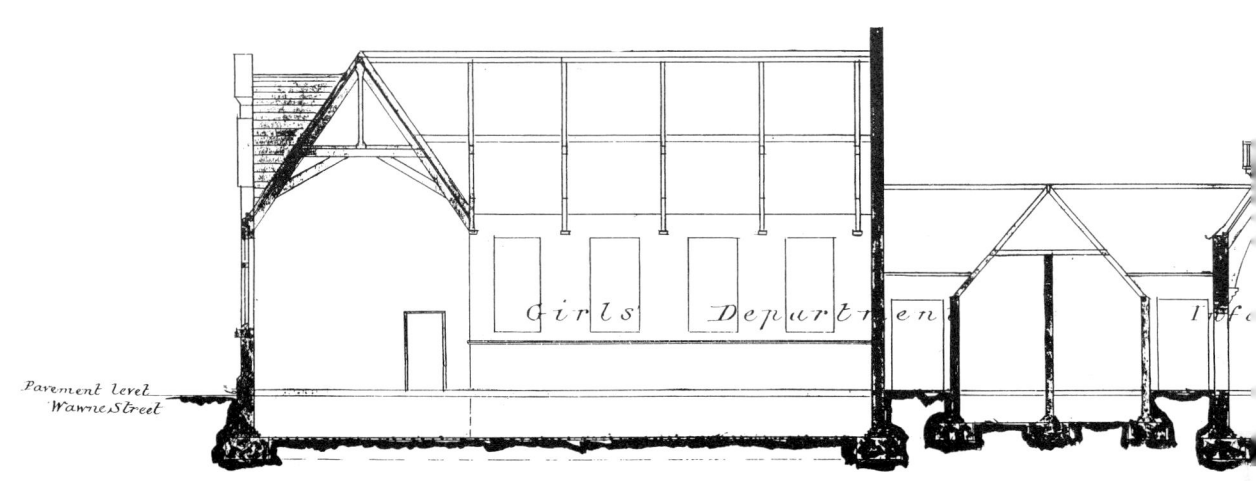

Pavement level
Wawne Street

Sectio.

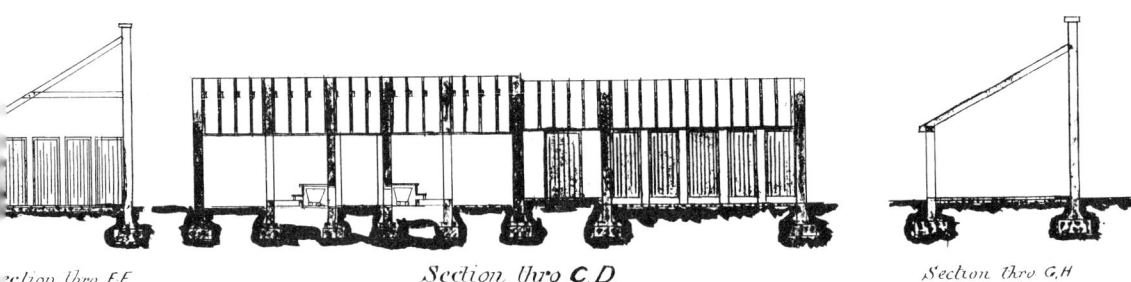

Section thro EF   Section thro C.D   Section thro G.H

Fig. 18.
Wawne
Street Board
School, one
of the first
College an-
nexes.
(KHRO)

Healing Chamber
(gallery over)

Department   Boys   Department

floor line   floor line

Pavement of Alexandra Street

A.B

A County Advisory Committee for Flour Milling was established by the Yorkshire Council for Further Education in 1929 with Riley as Joint Hon. Secretary.

Bates praised the work of the Yorkshire Council for Further Education as it had allowed advanced students from Goole and Beverley to be concentrated in Hull and its reports had saved considerable time and money. However, in 1933 the Hull Education Committee refused to pay the YCFE its £89 annual payment but would still co-operate with the Council "providing it did not involve any expenditure."[22] The Education Committee only resumed membership in 1944 at a fee of £100.

The Board of Education reported on the provision of technical education in Hull in April 1928. Hull Technical College and the School of Commerce served the East Riding and North Lincolnshire with an estimated population of 40 000 potential students. Six full time day students and 242 evening students attended the Colleges from outside Hull during the year. During the day 31 full time and 31 part time students were in the senior department at Park Street

Fig. 19. E. Percy Bates (HC)

and 595 in the Junior School. In the evening 1556 students attended science and technology courses and 454 women attended domestic classes. Besides these 225 students (flourmilling, tailor's cutting, butchers and grocers) had to be taught at Wawne Street and the YPI and 191 girls and women at the Day Street School. One hundred and fifteen teachers and 20 assistants were employed for the evening classes.

The Report did not think much of the Park Street building. *"The College is an unimpressive two storey building, solidly constructed, and containing a number of fairly large rooms. Its internal condition is somewhat dingy and depressing and the ventilation is defective."*[23] [By 1913 Park Street had been painted dark green and brown, which was expected to last at least 20 years.]

The Engineering Department suffered from lack of space and old, heavy, outdated equipment in the laboratories and workshops. The Building Department was one of the largest in the provinces and although much valuable work had been done the present accommodation was neither suitable nor adequate. The practical instruction to woodcutting machinists had to be given in a room formed out of a boilerhouse and the plumber's shop was used as the gymnasium during the day. The dark room used by the Physics Department had been constructed from a small space next to the boiler room, reached by a ladder, this made delicate experiments in spectroscopic work impossible.

The Natural Sciences Department did not have a laboratory at all for their pharmacy students. The Report recommended a greatly enlarged or, preferably, a new Technical College.

The School of Commerce suffered from being used as a Central School during the day and having no specialised equipment, such as a library or common rooms. The sanitary provision for women students was unacceptable. The headmaster also had to teach in the Junior School in Park Street during the day; the Report suggested that he be made full time at the School of Commerce. There was no provision of day commercial courses for girls in Hull due to a lack of accommodation. The Report considered a separate Commercial College essential.

There were no day time courses for women in domestic or trade subjects and the evening was not usually a very suitable time for older women. The rooms in the evening institutes were only makeshift and the Cookery Centres were equipped for school children only. The Report recommended a separate Institute for Women.

The Report concluded, *"It is evident that much valuable and effective work has been, and is being accomplished, but it is equally clear that the facilities for technical education now available in Hull lag behind the standard of modern requirements and fall far short of even present needs, while provision for future developments cannot be made without considerable additions to the premises now in use."*[24]

In June 1929 number 25 Park Street was purchased for £961 to relieve pressure on the Technical College to be used for the natural science department. The large room on the ground floor was converted into a pharmaceutical laboratory in 1935. An adjoining house, 26 Park Street, was purchased in 1930/31 the ground floor housed a science laboratory and brickwork shop for the building department and the first floor contained two rooms for senior students and the start of a reference library. The top floor connected with the next door house and made an extension for lithography and photolithography. A serious fire occurred in the annexe at 25 Park Street in January 1932 that severely damaged the workshop of the Watchmakers' Class.

Although a new building for the College had been promised Mr Bates still had to struggle with the unsatisfactory conditions at Park Street, as he reported to the education committee in 1929. *"The state of the Technical College is worse than ever and it has been necessary to turn out of the College additional courses in Plumbing, Sanitary Science, Wood Machinists, Press Tool Engineering and Upholstery, since rooms were not available to accommodate them. I regret the increasing tendency for these organised courses to become divorced from the College workshops."*[25]

THE NEW COLLEGE SITE

In July 1931 land became available for building on the Queen's Dock Estate and the Hull Education Committee decided they should be allocated a plot for the new technical college. By November 1932 they had earmarked three pieces of land containing 15630 sq. yds., 2320 sq. yds. and 920 sq. yds. a total of around 18870 sq. yds. In 1934 the Board of Education and the Ministry of Health approved the appropriation of the site for educational purposes. The Hull Education Committee had proposed to use an existing building on the site as a motor laboratory in 1934.

In 1935 Bates thought the new college would be built on the 3½ acre site in two years time. The science of aeronautics was to figure prominently in the curriculum and the new college would have its own hangers and aeroplanes. By 1938/39 the site had expanded to 8½ acres with the Board of Education contributing

Fig. 20. Park Street late 1920s or early '30s, externally the premises had changed very little since 1898 (KHRO)

Fig. 21. Blitz damage to Park Street (HC)

Australia, Canada or other portions of the British Dominions."[26]

A couple of years later the workshops for plumbing, welding and engineering students were strongly criticised by A. B. Crawford, the HM Inspector of factories in Hull, who said they would not be tolerated in any factory.

THE SECOND WORLD WAR

Frank Walker was appointed Head of the Mathematics Department at the Technical College in 1939. Later in the year W. Cooper, Head of Riley, died and pending the erection of the new Riley High School, Mr Walker was made Vice-Principal of the Technical College and given responsibility for Riley under the general control of the Principal, Mr Bates.

On three occasions the windows of the Technical College at Park Street suffered blast damage but in May 1941 it was unfortunate enough to receive two parcels of incendiary bombs. Despite the united efforts of the firewatchers, women trainees and the A.F.S. the roof and top storey of the greater part of the building were

50% of the costs. In contrast Birmingham had recently erected a college on 5½ acres and Sheffield was putting a new educational centre on only 3½ acres.

In 1939, the Old Boy's Association asked the Hull Education Committee to name part of the new technical college after Mr Luxton, Luxton had died the previous year in Minehead at the age of 76. A series of test bores were made for the new buildings in 1940 but the

war led to the abandonment of the scheme.

Bates continued to criticise the lack of facilities at the Technical College and in 1936 said: *"Had the authorities in Hull 40 years ago had the wisdom to provide proper facilities for education this would have been a far finer industrial city today.*

Even now citizens of Hull have worse facilities than any other city of its size in the United Kingdom, destroyed. Almost immediately Mr Bates set about the work of demolition and reconstruction. He organised the staff and senior students into groups for various types of work to such good purpose that within a week the trainees were at their normal work. Besides acting as general supervisor of the re-roofing, Mr Bates took an active part on the top of the building removing the dangerous sections and later with barrow and shovel set the pace in removing debris. Without his courage and leadership the Technical College would have been declared derelict. Apart from the loss of the engineering drawing offices, chemistry laboratories and a few classrooms the whole of the College reopened in the September although the Boulevard School had to be used to enable the work of the College to carry on without interruption.

The cost of reconstructing the College was estimated at £5000 on buildings and £500 on furniture in 1943. A further £12000 was provided for the emergency reconstruction of the College for 1947/48.

Fig. 22. Printing Department, Room 31 (F4), Mr Bates is on the right. A photocopier currently occupies this space. (HC)

BATES RETIRES

E. P. Bates submitted his resignation in May 1942 to take effect from 31 August 1942. Hull Education Committee reluctantly accepted his resignation but in the circumstances persuaded him to be reappointed as temporary Acting Principal from 2 September 1942. He gave £50 and dies and a stock of medals for the endowment of an annual award of a medal at the College. Bates retired from 1 September 1944 and F. Walker, aged 53, was appointed to succeed him as temporary Acting Principal. Frank Walker had been at the College for 32 years but only reluctantly took charge. Frank received the nickname 'Johnnie' Walker as he often repeated the phrase 'born 1820 and still going strong'. Edwin Harrison, Assistant Master and a former pupil at the College, became the temporary Acting Vice-Principal. Harrison was nicknamed 'Tiger' and his bite was said to be worse than his bark.

At Mr Bate's retirement ceremony in 1944 Alderman Holmes praised his achievements stating that they had been in the worst possible of buildings. He hoped that the work Mr Bates had pioneered and put on a sound footing, would be intensified in the 'new building'.

Mr Walker paid tribute to Mr Bates in the 1944/45 College Year Book. Bates had been educated at Hull Grammar School and became a pupil teacher at the New Holland National School before training as a teacher at St John's College, Battersea. He then spent two years as a certificated assistant in the London schools and in 1902 returned to Hull as English Master at the Craven Street Secondary School. The following year Bates was appointed English Master at the Technical College. In 1919 he became Headmaster of the Central School of Commerce that he built up to become a large and efficient evening school of some 1000 students.

Bates was responsible for establishing, and finding accommodation for, the Bakery, Dental Mechanics and Motor Car Engineering courses at Hessle Road; the Trawler Engineers on St Andrew's Dock; the Wood Cutting Machinists at Williamson Street School. At one time The Technical College day and evening class courses were spread over eight buildings. Bates firmly believed that given adequate equipment keen students would always attend although the building lacked even reasonable comforts.

Mr Bates took particular interest in the Printing Department, as the excellent quality of the College produced Year Books from 1930 show. The department was well equipped and from 1933 the Museums and Art Gallery Committee allowed it to reproduce original pictures from the Corporation's collection many of which appeared in the Year Books.

Notes for Chapter Two

1. J. Lang, City & Guilds of London Institute, 1878-1978.
2. T. Bamford, The University of Hull, 1978.
3. Minutes of The Hull Education Committee, 27 January 1908.
4. T. Bamford, The University of Hull, 1978.
5. Principal's Report to H.E.C. 1910-11
6. Minutes of The Hull Education Committee, 21 November 1911.
7. Ibid., 13 April 1915.
8. Ibid., 14 May 1918.
9. Ibid.
10. Hull Daily Mail, 18 November 1918.
11. Ibid., 26 November 1918.
12. Eastern Morning News, 29 November 1918.
13. Minutes of Hull Education Committee, 10 December 1918.
14. Ibid., 7 February 1922.
15. T. Bamford, The University of Hull, 1978.
16. Minutes of Hull Education Committee, 11 April 1922.
17. Ibid., 9 June 1925.
18. Ibid., 14 June 1921.
19. Principal's Report to the H.E.C. 1922-23.
20. Ibid.
21. Principal's Report to the H.E.C. 1925-26.
22. Minutes of Hull Education Committee, 14 March 1933.
23. Report of H.M.I. on the Provision of Technical Education in Hull, 1928.
24. Ibid.
25. Minutes of Hull Education Committee, 15 October 1929.
26. Hull Daily Mail, 8 April 1936.

CONSEQUENCES OF THE 1944 EDUCATION ACT

"The annual intake into the industries of the country of men trained by universities and technical colleges, has been and still is, insufficient both in quantity and quality ... In part, the experience of the war has shown that the greatest deficiency in British industry is the shortage of scientists and technologists who can administer and organise and can apply the results of research to development."[1]

However the 1943 Government White Paper on Educational Reconstruction had surprisingly paid little attention to remedying the problem (technical, commercial and art education only occupied a page and a half of the Paper) and envisaged spending only £2.49 millions on technical education in the first seven years of the proposed programme compared with £17 millions on nursery schools. Many educationalists at the time saw this as a lack of commitment to the development of the technical college sector.

Technical education eventually became an integral part of further education under the direction of the Ministry of Education and the Local Education Authority as a result of the 1944 Education Act. Each LEA now had a duty to provide technical education, not simply a right, that the authority could exercise at its own discretion. Unfortunately the Act was still vague when it came to setting out how technical education should be developed. A new system of County Colleges was proposed where employees under 18 would have to attend to receive further education, including physical, practical and vocational training but the Act did not make clear how the functions of these new colleges were to be separated from existing technical colleges. The scheme was reminiscent of the proposals in Fisher's Act of 1918 for compulsory further education.

It used to be assumed that universities would produce scientists and technologists and the technical colleges would train technicians and skilled craftsmen. This had ceased to be the case by the end of the Second World War and in 1944 the Ministry of Education set-up a committee on Higher Technical Education under Lord Percy. The Percy Report came out in 1945 recommending that a small number of the larger technical colleges teach more courses to university standard with their elementary courses moved elsewhere. The government accepted these recommendations and created Colleges of Technology.

The 1944 Education Act had required all Local Education Authorities to produce a development plan for education. Hull Council issued its Scheme of Further Education and Plan for County Colleges in 1948. In the scheme the Council anticipated that the number of people who would be eligible to receive further education would not show any marked change within following five years.

The scheme gave a breakdown of existing facilities for vocational education that included the Technical College, Nautical College and the Colleges of Art and Commerce and three independently controlled combined branch technical and commercial evening institutes in Flinton Street, Welton Street and Riley High Schools. It also gave statistics on the numbers attending courses at the

Technical College in 1946/47. In the full time day department there were 438 students:

Engineering
BSc (Engineering)	24
HND Mech. Eng.	21

with Aeronautical Endorsement

Ministry of Transport Certificates in Marine Engineering:
Second Class	47
First Class	19
Extra Chief's	1
Endorsements	4

City & Guilds Certificate in Radio Eng. 3

Chemistry
BSc (Chemistry)	65

Pharmacy:
Inter B Pharm
Pharmaceutical Society	12

Apothecaries Hall

Building
OND	13

Radio Operating
Postmaster General's Certificates:
Special Certificate
Second Class	137

First Class
Aircraft Certificate

Sanitary Inspection
Royal Sanitary Institute & Sanitary Inspector's Exam.	26

Pre-nursing
Part I, Exam of General Nursing Council	38

Most of the part time day students attended day classes as part of grouped courses for the remainder of which they also attended evening classes. The part time day courses were as follows:

Engineering
BSc (Engineering)	5
HND Mech. Eng.	1
ONC Mech. Eng.	11
ONC Elect. Eng.	9
Trawler Eng.	20
Welding	2

Chemistry
BSc (Chemistry)	37

Pharmacy:
Apothecaries Society	2
Pharmaceutical Society	8

Building
HNC	10
ONC	35
City & Guilds certificate in Brickwork	108
C & G certificate in Carpentry and Joinery	208
C & G Plumbing	42
C & G Woodcutting machinists	8
C & G Gasfitting	13

Printing
C & G Typography	5
C & G Letterpress machinists work	6

In the part time evening (grouped) classes there were 2793 students taking courses in engineering, chemistry, building, sanitary inspectors, paint technology, seed crushing, furniture trades, printing trades, dentistry, flour-milling, bakery, meat trades and grocery. In the part time evening (separate subjects) classes there were 405 students with courses in engineering, radio, printing trades, nursing, natural science, leather technology, hairdressing, industrial administration (foreman) and grocery.

Statistics were also given on the intake of the Technical College of students from outside of the Hull area:

%	Total No. of Students	E Riding	W Riding	Lindsey	Other Areas
Full time courses	438	86	4	2	109
Part time (day)	530	67	1	1	-
Part time evening (grouped)	2739	478	45	2	1
Part time evening (separate subjects)	405	54	-	-	-

It was assumed that the new Hull colleges would still attract some students from Goole, Selby and Lindsey but the numbers were not expected to increase significantly except in marine engineering and wireless operators courses.

Fig. 23. Abercrombie Plan produced for Hull City Council showing the proposed new technical schools, 1945

The Hull Scheme proposed a group of Central Colleges (i.e. Technical, Commercial, Art and a new College for Adult Education) linked with four independently controlled branch colleges; branch colleges would provide courses for students up to 18, who would be able to pass to the more advanced studies at the Central Colleges. The branch colleges would be sited on the outskirts of the city on 20 acre sites, each with a County College (County Colleges were recommended by the 1944 Education Act for the provision of compulsory further education for 15-18 year olds not otherwise receiving formal education; they were never implemented) accommodating 450 students per day as its nucleus. Each branch college would have to make provision for:

- County College courses
- Voluntary evening courses
- Youth activities in evenings and weekends
- Voluntary day and part time evening courses
- Authorised courses for unemployed people under 18 if and when required.

The population in Hull of 15 to 18 year olds was estimated to be 13,079 and of these only 700 would be exempt from attending the county colleges at some time during that period. To cope with the expected large number of students some provision had to be made at the new central colleges for specialist training it would be uneconomical to set-up at the county colleges. At the Central Technical College this would involve 2588 students attending for one day per week.

The Scheme also proposed *"that the ultimate goal will be that the group of central colleges and associated buildings shall form a unified whole, and become a responsible single academic institution. The Authority is desirous that in the interest of the students the institution shall develop in that it will be in a position to achieve university status or a status comparable to that of a university"*.[2]

Included in the group of buildings at the central colleges would be a common block designed to house the library of the Colleges and student union room, halls, refectory, kitchens, etc. The Nautical College was not to be moved to Queen's Gardens at the request of the local fishing industry who thought it should be sited near the docks.

At the new Technical College new courses were proposed in chemical engineering, biochemical analysis, slating and tiling, masonry and pre-cast stonework, radar, boilerhouse practice, cinematograph technicians, meat processing, milk technology and catering (trade and housecraft courses). Also the courses in tailor's cutting, watch and clock making and furniture trades that had been suspended during the war were to be resumed. Existing courses in motor car engineering, electrical installation bakery and confectionery and hairdressing were to be developed. The Scheme proposed a student capacity of 1600 in attendance at any one time.

Two junior technical schools for girls were planned and the existing junior technical schools were to be rehoused as technical high schools of engineering, building, commerce, art and crafts and nautical training. Riley High School would be moved to the Boulevard.

At the secondary high school level Newton Hall and Kelvin Hall were created as mixed technical high schools, not related to any particular occupation but providing a general education with science and its applications as the core, in combination with modern schools on a campus. Kelvin Hall, opened in 1959, originally had accommodation for 600 pupils and, with Wyke Hall mixed secondary modern school, formed Bricknell High School. Newton Hall, opened in 1957, also accommodated 600 pupils and with Elizabeth Hall and Shakespeare Hall formed Greatfield High School. The four high schools attached to the colleges, technical, commercial, art and nautical were to be further developed. Trinity House Navigational School was to be a technical high school. It was hoped that these schools would be able to provide a supply of students to the County and Central Colleges.

Adult education was also to be well provided for. The Authority aimed to establish, as part of the central colleges on the Queen's Gardens site, a central college for adult education with adequate facilities for liberal studies with a capacity of 600 students and it was hoped that the college would be an inspiration for cultural activities in the city as a whole. The Authority also wanted to establish a residential college for further education accommodating 30 students at a country house in pleasant surroundings.

The Authority was also asked to supply a building programme for the next 5 years and decided that the Central Technical College and the County Colleges should be built first:

Central Technical College
Queen's Gardens   £1,175,000
Western County College
Beverley Rd., Hessle   200 000
North Western C.C.
Priory Road   200 000
Northern C.C.
Sutton Road   200 000
Eastern C.C.
Marfleet Lane   200 000

The Ministry of Education approved the decision to build the new Central Colleges on the Queen's Gardens site in June 1949. F. Gibberd was appointed as architect for the new Technical College (the first to be built) in December 1949. The Ministry approved the whole of the Scheme of Further Education and the Plan for County Colleges in May 1953 subject to certain reservations and it deferred detailed consideration of the Plan for County Colleges *"until such time as it is expedient to review all such plans".*[3]

The County College system was never introduced (and hence the Branch Colleges were also not built) and this caused Hull problems later on as they had relied on the County College sites taking on most of the junior work of the Colleges for Further Education (i.e. the existing colleges of Commerce, Technical, Art and Nautical).

DEVELOPMENTS AT THE TECHNICAL COLLEGE DURING THE 1940s AND '50s

Fees in secondary schools were abolished and the school leaving age raised to 15 in 1944 and further increased to 16 in 1973-4. No fees were paid for any pupil under 19 at any of the Hull Colleges of Further Education (including the Technical College) from 1945.

The roles of the separate Elementary and Higher Education Subcommittees of Hull City Council were combined in a new Schools and Colleges Subcommittee, of the Education Committee, from

November 1945 with Alderman Lister as Chairman.

It was proposed, in 1946, to separate Riley High School and the High School for Engineering (two of the Technical College's junior schools) from the Technical College from 1947 to form one school. Riley finally left Park Street, twenty years after it had first been proposed, moving to the Boulevard school vacated when Kingston High School moved to new premises. E. Harrison was appointed temporary Acting Head Master of Riley and the High School for Engineering from 1 April 1945. Herbert Rochester, of Kenilworth, became the Head Master of the independently administered Riley High School from October 1947.

Canteen facilities were provided at the Park Street site from the beginning of 1949. The Technical College also rented premises in Canning Street around 1945 although it is not clear what they were used for.

Room 2 (now reception) at the Park Street site was partitioned to provide a separate Principal's Room in 1953/4. The gate and railings were also reinstated in 1954 after being removed during the war. These utilitarian railings are themselves probably due for replacement.

Common rooms were provided for Park Street and Queen's Gardens students in 1958; an upper room was rented at 23 Park Street and vacant premises at 9a Dock Office Row (Bestobel House) were acquired. Bell's Asbestos & Engineering Ltd. had terminated their tenancy of Bestobel House and the Committee took possession in May 1953. The common room at Dock Office Row was extended in 1963 and the ground floor of the building was also used by the College.

Frank Walker was eventually appointed Principal of the Technical College in November 1949 (he had been Acting Principal since Mr Bates retired) and resigned a year and a half later. He had been a teacher from 1912 until 1919 when he started at the College. It was proposed to replace the Principal of the Technical College with a Principal of the whole new

Fig. 24. Bestobel House, Dock Office Row, 1993. (CJK)

College for Further Education (a combination of the colleges of Commerce, Art, Technical and Adult Education) later on. Walker was asked to extend his services until August 1951 when a successor should have been appointed. E. Harrison had to take charge of the College from the September until the October when a new Principal was selected. There were seven candidates of which only one, H. Rochester, was from Hull; Emlyn Jones, aged 43, of Whitley Bay was appointed on a starting salary of £1450. Jones was a first class honours graduate from Leeds University and his first teaching post had been in Liverpool as a chemistry lecturer. He then became Head of the chemistry and biology department at Rutherford College of Technology, Newcastle in 1947.

One of Mr Jones's first official functions, in 1951, as the new Principal of the Technical College was a dinner at the Hull Centre of the Institute of the Motor Industry where he asked the industry for advice on equipment for the new college. At that function he also called technical education the Cinderella of education that had too often been taken to the palace gates only to be relegated again to the back kitchen.

BUILDING THE FIRST PART OF THE NEW TECHNICAL COLLEGE

There were proposals to build temporary office accommodation, to last seven years, in 1946 on the Queen's Gardens site (that had been allocated for the new Technical College since 1933) but these were rejected as the building of the new Technical College was to be commenced *"without delay"*.[4]

In August 1947 the Hull Education Committee proposed to erect temporary huts on the Queen's Gardens site for the Building Trades Department. This was revised soon after to include huts for the new Art College as well. The Ministry of Education approved the scheme but the Education Committee decided to acquire additional land on Salthouse Lane and build the huts for the Building Science, Junior and Senior Brickwork Section and Plumbers' and Plasterers' Shops there instead. The work had to start by the end of March 1951 or funding would be lost. The huts were built on College Circle, which was a roundabout between Queen's Gardens and the present College that disappeared in subsequent road alterations.

The Corporation submitted the first instalment of the new Technical College at Queen's Gardens as part of its building programme for 1952/53, however, the Ministry did not give its approval but said they would consider it for the following year if amended. A special sub-committee of the Hull Education Committee urged the Ministry to reconsider and they successfully reinstated the building programme.

The Ministry of Education approved the sum of £270,000 in the building programme to erect the first instalment of the new Technical College - the workshop block - for the 1952/53 session. William Moss & Sons of Loughborough won the tender to build the workshop block for £318,793; although this was the lowest tender it still exceeded the spending limit by over £76,000. Moss reduced his tender further to £311,998 a few months later.

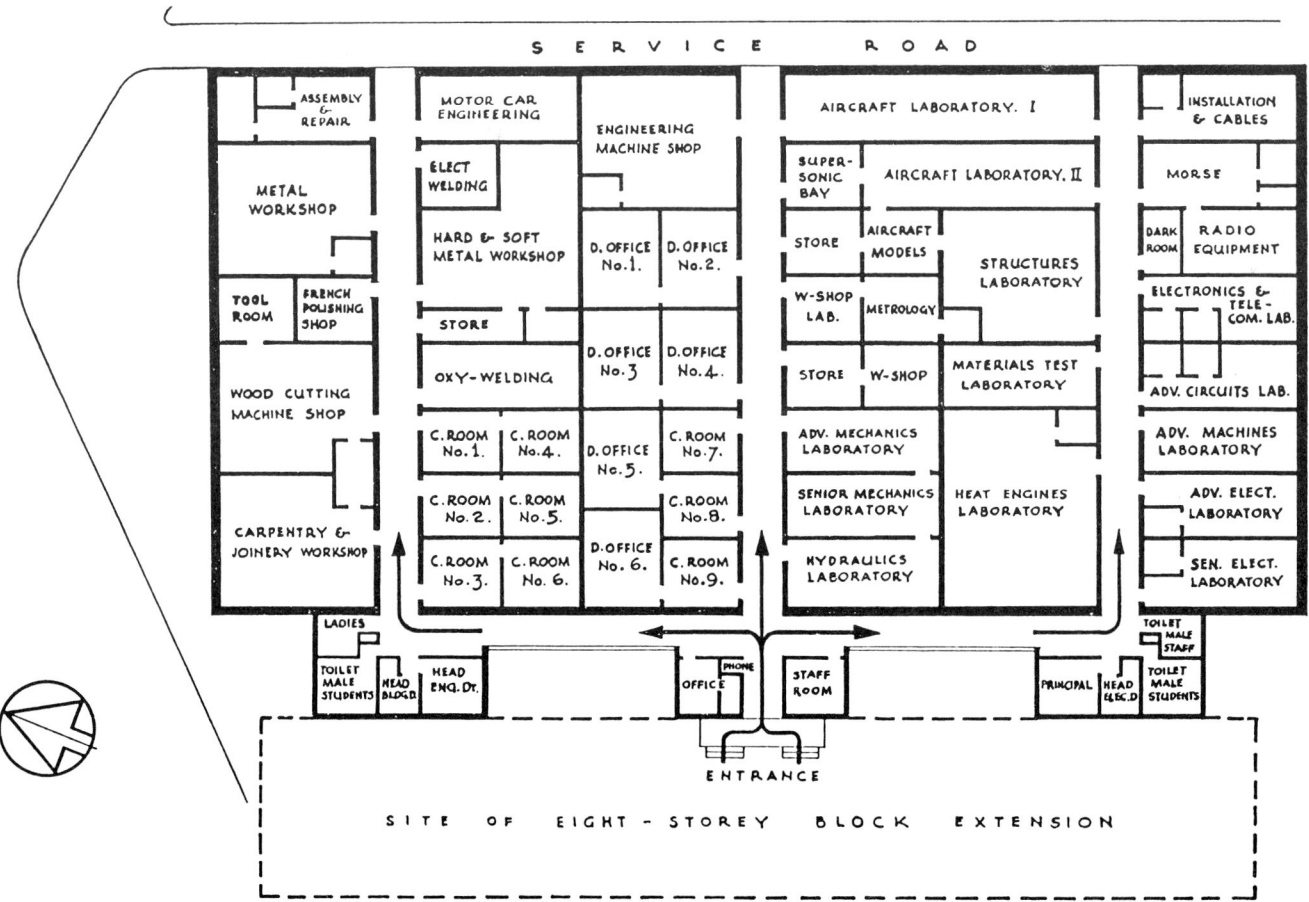

Fig. 25. Plan of the new Workshops, 1956 (HC)

A commemorative stone was laid at the new site in 1952 by Councillor Lionel Rosen, Sheriff of Hull, old Technicalian and President of the Technical College and Riley High School Old Boys' Association. The Chairman of Rolls Royce and the National Council for Technological Awards, Lord Hives, officially opened the Workshop Block in 1956. At the opening Lord Hives urged the Education Committee to be bold. *"Technical education is a topical subject today. It is freely discussed at all levels, and there is complete agreement about the necessity for it.*

I am always suspicious when there is complete agreement, because that often happens at the time when nothing gets done. We need the bar of disagreement to stimulate action, so I would recommend to your Education Committee - be ambitious on your outlook and don't be put off."[5]

The final cost of the first instalment amounted to £370, 489/ 2s but the original loan sanction had been only £353, 945 an excess expenditure of £16, 544/ 2s.

The Technical College officially changed its name to the Hull Col-

Fig. 26. The Workshop Block, c1962 (HC)

lege of Technology from September 1955 although its status remained the same.

The Old Boys Association suggested adding the words "Scientia Potentas est" to a new crest to be fitted to the wall beside the main entrance to the workshop block. The motto translates freely as 'knowledge is power' and was used by the new College of Technology.

In October 1952 fire destroyed the printing shop, plumbers shop and engineering science laboratory in Park Street; the printing department moved to the new Queen's Gardens site. The College claimed £6650 for equipment lost in the fire.

THE 1956 EDUCATION WHITE PAPER

The next major piece of legislation to affect the College was the White Paper of 1956 which concentrated on the provision of advanced courses. The Paper made up for the vagueness of the 1944 Act and envisaged a large increase in the number of students attending advanced courses at technical colleges; it also wanted to see a doubling of the students released by employers for day courses. Before the Second World War employers were reluctant to release their workers for part time day courses and nationally there were only 42,000 day release students in 1938. The war had shown the value of an educated workforce and in 1957 there were 417,000 day release students. The Paper proposed an expansion of sandwich courses but only in those colleges *"which concentrate on advanced courses of technological level."*[6]

In its introduction the Paper stated that *"technical education must not be too narrowly vocational or too confined to one skill or trade. Swift change is the characteristic of our age, so that a main purpose of the technical education of the future must be to teach boys and girls to be adaptable. Versatility has been the aim of a classical education; technical studies should lead to a similar versatility and should, therefore, be firmly grounded on the fundamentals of mathematics and science. It is much easier to adopt new ideas and new techniques when the principles on which they are based are already familiar."*[7] The White Paper also stressed the importance of liberal studies in technical education.

The National Council of Technology had been established in 1948 to see if internally administered degree level courses could replace the external University of London examinations. In 1955, under the chairmanship of Lord Hives, the National Council for Technological Awards was set-up to control a new award, the Diploma in Technology, which was awarded as a result of 4/5 year sandwich courses. The new award was introduced in 1957 and 10 Colleges of Advanced Technology were created.

After 1957 technical colleges were classified as Colleges of Advanced Technology, Regional Colleges or Area Colleges. CAT's taught only advanced courses; Regional Colleges taught both advanced and lower level courses but concentrated more on the higher level and Area Colleges taught mainly lower level courses with some advanced work, mainly part time (the distinction between Regional and Area colleges was very blurred). To become a CAT or a Regional College it was an advantage for an existing college to receive an Advanced Technology Grant. Hull College of Technology applied for the grant for four of its courses in 1957 - though it had been available since 1952 - and was refused. A Ministry of Education Circular stated that *"courses in advanced technology are not likely to thrive except in an institution which has a high standard of accommodation and equipment"*.[8] Unfortunately Park Street did not meet this description and by the time the new main block on Queen's Gardens was completed the grant was no longer available.

The vagueness on the provision of high level courses led to what the Secretary of State for Education & Science described as *"a continuous rat-race to reach the First or University Division"*.[9] If every college achieving high standards moved automatically into the University Club the remaining public sector colleges would become *"a permanent poor relation perpetually deprived of its brightest ornaments and with a permanently and openly inferior status"*.[10] The Secretary of State also urged colleges *"To strive for their own excellence rather than copy the Joneses or try to change their name"*.[11]

Hostels for students from outside Hull studying at the Hull College of Technology were proposed in principle in 1957 and 1960 but never developed although they were initially included in the 1963/64 building programme. Perhaps the Hull Education Committee thought the hostels could boost the College's claim for more advanced courses by attracting high level, full time students.

The sluggish economy of Hull during the 1950s was also not in the College's favour. Unemployment was higher than the national average throughout the 1950s and the chemical and building industries were not expanding at the same rate as in other areas.

CHANGES IN GOVERNMENT OF THE HULL COLLEGES

In 1956 the Hull Education Committee produced proposals for new Governing Bodies for each of the four Colleges of Further Education. An earlier 1948 Plan proposed that only members of the Education Committee should be included but a Committee member put down an amendment that they should consist of 15 members 10 of who would be members of the Education Committee together with 5 persons nominated by industrial, commercial, technical, professional and University interests. The Governing Bodies were to be sub-committees of the Education Committee. However, this amendment was lost and when the governing bodies were set-up only members of the Colleges and Schools Subcommittee were represented. In 1946 the Ministry of Education had suggested that colleges should have strong governing bodies with representatives of industrial and commercial interests and the universities as well as the LEA. Such bodies were to have *"all reasonable freedom of action in directing the affairs of the College"*[12] so that they might

"develop its work in such directions as prove desirable" and *"attract first class teachers on to the staff"*.[13]

The new Governing Body of the Hull College of Technology first meet on 11 June 1957 with Councillor Schultz as Chairman and Councillor Rosen as Deputy Chairman. The Body lacked any independence and rather complacently thought that its system of advisory committees constituted an adequate method of representing outside concerns. The other colleges (i.e. Commerce, Art and Nautical) had equally inadequate Governing Bodies.

The Hull Education Committee slightly relaxed its sole control of the Governing Bodies from the municipal year 1961/62. The Hull Incorporated Chamber of Commerce and Shipping and the Hull Trades Council were each invited to nominate two people and the University was invited to nominate one person to serve as co-optative members.

After a visit by HM Inspectors in 1962 the existing Advisory Committees were discontinued and replaced with new ones on bakery & confectionery, building, electrical engineering, mechanical engineering, food technologies, furniture trades, hairdressing, management studies (jointly with the College of Commerce), printing, science & mathematics. The old Advisory Committees had contained representatives of industry and commerce but the Governing Body of the College of Technology (i.e. Hull City Councillors) had used their presence as an excuse not to elect outside agencies to the Governing Body. The undemocratic nature of the Governing body had an adverse effect when the College bided for Polytechnic status.

In 1970 the Department of Education and Science recommended that Governing Bodies of colleges should not have a majority of Local Authority members; the Governing Body of the Hull College of Technology certainly had to be altered, as most of its members were Councillors, and in 1972 a new Body with 24 members was formed with:

9 representatives of the Hull LEA
1 from the East Riding LEA
6 from commerce and industry
1 from the Academic Board of the College

1 member of the College teaching staff
2 from the University of Hull
1 head teacher from a Senior High School
1 co-opted member able to make some special contribution
The Principal.

The Academic Board of the College, whose establishment had been recommended in 1967, should have places for the Principal, Vice-Principal, Heads of Departments, Chief Administration Officer, the Librarian and a certain number of teaching staff. *"Subject to the overall responsibility of the Governors the Academic Board shall be responsible for the planning, co-ordination, development and oversight of the academic work of the College including arrangement for the admission and examination of students."*[14]

BUILDING THE MAIN BLOCK OF THE COLLEGE

During the 1950s many annexes were still in use by the College of Technology as neither Park Street nor the new Queen's Gardens workshops could cope with student demands, they included;

Osborne Street (building)
Middleton Street (aeronautics)
Salthouse Lane (brickwork)
Hessle Road (bakery)
St Marks Street (N E Gas Board)
Beverley Road (hairdressing)
Williamson Street (workshops)
Wilberforce High School, Leicester Street, and
Queen's Gardens annexe.

Hull Education Committee wanted to purchase extra land for the new college but the Ministry of Town and Country Planning, in 1953, did not think that any development could take place on acquisition of land for the new college bounded by Clifford Street, Dock Street and George Street for the next five years. The site eventually became the new police station.

Gibberd, the Architect (who, incidentally, had been responsible for Liverpool's Roman Catholic Cathedral and Harlow New Town), estimated that the cost of building the main block of the new Technical College, in front of the existing workshops, would be £750,000 and the Corporation included it in its building programme for 1955/56. However, the Ministry refused to allocate the scheme any money for that year and a deputation from the Education Committee saw the Minister when she visited Hull in November 1954. The appeal was successful and the Ministry considered the scheme and approved it provided work could start before the end of March 1956. However, in March 1955 the Ministry regretted that in the light of available capital resources it had been unable to include the second instalment in the 1955/56 programme but would consider it for the following year.

The second instalment (main block) of the new College of Technology was included in Hull Council's building programme for 1956/57 at £642,004. Spooner's (Hull) Ltd won the tender to build the new block for £761,884 although the Ministry of Education could only sanction a loan for £673,900. All new and transferred machinery was to be painted light blue at the suggestion of the architect. The mural over the entrance was designed and made by William Mitchell & Associates unfortunately the protective coating was not successful and the mural had to be refaced in 1964. The mural represents the nautical associations of the site and also incorporates mathematical and nautical symbols. Work started in

early September 1957 and the first students occupied the building from 18 September 1961. The final cost of the main block was £872 766 16s 4d but only £837 100 had been raised in loans. Alderman J. L. Schultz officially opened the building on 14 May 1962 and the opening ceremony was also attended by Frank Walker of Keyingham and E. Percy Bates of Driffield, both former

Fig. 27. St Mark's Street Annexe entrance (HC)

Fig. 28. Construction of the Main Block (HC)

principals. Schultz was perhaps being over optimistic when he said, *"Today we see developed the first part of the educational scheme which will grace what will eventually be the finest city centre in the country."*[15]

The educational record of the College was favourably commented on as in the past few years it had secured for students 184 external degrees, 110 associateships of professional societies, 585 HNCs, 89 HNDs and 1007 certificates of competency in marine engineering.

When Hull had received permission to build the second instalment the Principal of Hull College of Technology, Mr Jones addressed the Old Boys' annual dinner and commented on the second rate nature of technical education. *"The Americans are training eight times as many technologists as we are although their population is only three times greater than ours. People in this country are not yet convinced of the need for expenditure in technical education. Victorian Traditions are holding us back."*[16]

The foundations for the new building needed to be very firm

Fig. 29. Opening of the Main Block (HC)

because of poor quality ground and are reinforced concrete piles which are founded in the boulder clay strata approximately 40ft below ground level. The piles are connected by pile caps and concrete beams which form the base for in situ reinforced concrete columns at 12ft centres. Floors and floor beams are also in reinforced concrete throughout. The end walls of the building are faced in reconstituted Portland Stone slabs.

The foundation of Wilberforce Monument needed strengthening due to the building work at a cost of £1600 and from 1960 the maintenance of the monument became the responsibility of the Education Committee.

A plaque in memory of the late E. H. Bullock was placed in the Lecture Hall of the new College in 1961. Bullock had been Town Clerk and was keen and diligent over the early negotiations for the

Fig. 30. Three Principals and Sir Leo Schultz at the opening ceremony (Walker, Bates, Schultz, Jones) (HC)

College; he had been a student at the College for four years and was President of the Old Boys' Association. There was also a plaque to record the occasion when Councillor Rosen laid the commemorative paving stone in the forecourt placed in the entrance foyer. Two years later the name plate 'Lecture Theatre II' on the door of room 715 was replaced by 'the Leonard Balmforth Lecture Theatre' in memory of the Head of the Chemistry Department who had recently died.

DEVELOPMENTS AT THE COLLEGE OF TECHNOLOGY DURING THE 1960s AND '70s

The post of Vice-Principal was created in 1959 and the head of the Physics Department, O. C. Gay, was appointed from October 1959. From 1 September 1965 Oliver Gay became the full time Vice-Principal.

The Principal, Mr Jones, was appointed a member of the National Advisory Council on Education for Industry and Commerce by the Ministry of Education in 1961. The Council's function was to advise the Minister on the national policy necessary for the full development of further education in relation to industry and commerce. He was also appointed a member of the Association of Principals of Technical Institutions in 1970.

The accommodation at Queen's Gardens was still inadequate, even after the main block had been built, for the numbers of students and Park Street had to be retained as an annexe. Park Street still had quite substantial amounts spent on improvements during the 1960s. Additional machinery and fitting shops were to cost £8000 in 1962/63 but this was later reduced to £2920; the electrical equipment at the annexe was changed from DC to AC current during 1962. Extra library facilities, a demonstration laboratory and a science laboratory were provided in 1964.

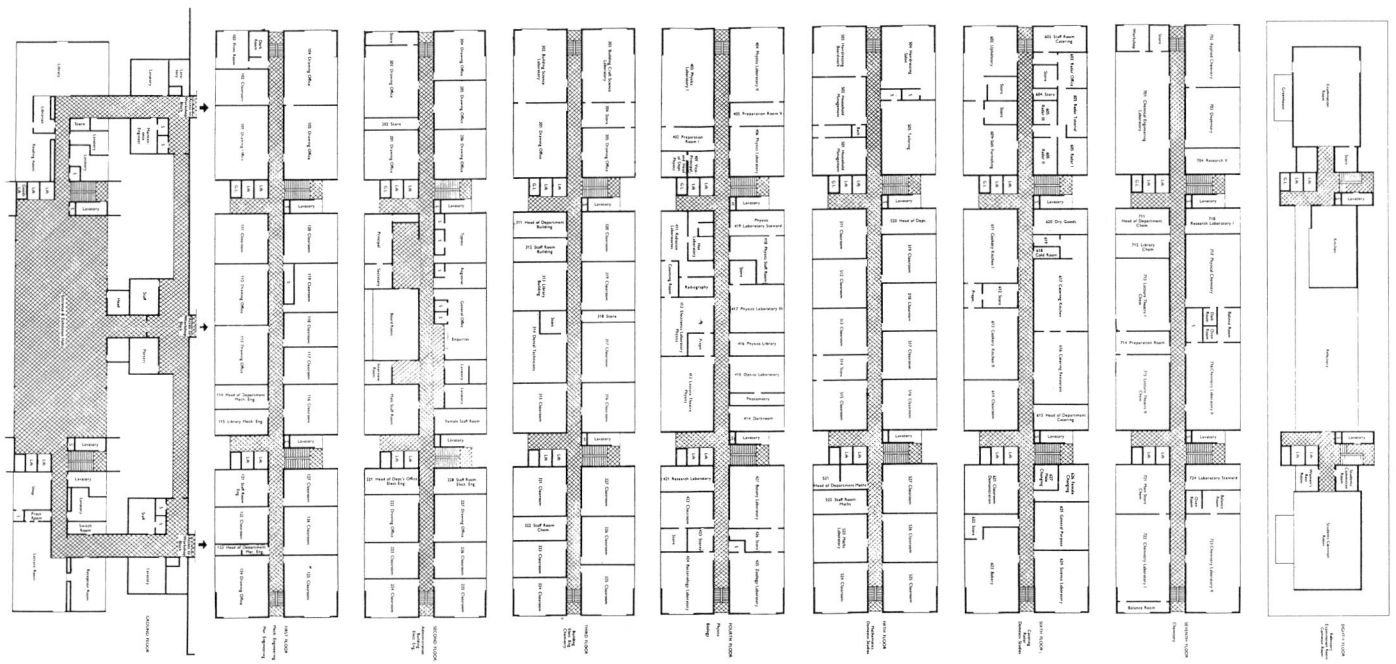

Fig. 31. The layout of the Main Block, 1962 (HC)

The Salthouse Lane annexe was improved slightly in 1961 with extra land, a new brick store and a wider entrance. A further piece of land was acquired for improvements to the annexe later in 1961.

The Charterhouse Lane High School and 1a Charterhouse Lane became annexes of the College from 1967. The science laboratories were used primarily by prenursing students; the remaining classrooms for Liberal Studies lectures and by the November there were facilities for art, drama and pottery. Other buildings were taken over as annexes over the next few years including The old Telephone House in Wincolmlee for additional workshop accommodation from 1968 until it was demolished for redevelopment. Some craft courses used premises of the Gas Board in St Mark's Street from September 1968. The upper floor of Crowle Street School was used from April 1970 and the whole building became occupied from 1970/71 to provide facilities for integrated courses of training for apprentices in the electrical contracting industry and in the motor trade.

The Sir Christopher Wren Technical High School, formerly the building junior school, was to become separated from the College from 1963 with new premises and a separate Head Master. An Acting Head was appointed in March 1965 although the school never moved from Osborne Street and closed in the late 1960s.

The College held a Science Fair and Open Week from 13-20 July 1963 organised by the British Association for the Advancement of Science. The fair was the largest held in the country and provided an exhibition of work by young people in school, college, local societies and industry. Speakers at the Fair pointed to the lack of electronics laboratories in the North and hoped this would soon be remedied.

Mr M. Collard of Nottingham was appointed Industrial Liaison Officer in October 1965. Hull College of Technology was one of only seven colleges selected to establish an Industrial Liaison Centre. The Centre was jointly established by the College and the Ministry of Technology and its purpose was to help industry, particularly the small and medium sized firms, make fuller use of existing technical information and to encourage technological innovations. The Department of Trade and Industry withdrew financial support for Industrial Liaison Centres from July 1973. The cost of the Centre was £5720 per year and the College agreed to fund it from 1973/74. The Centre became the responsibility of Hull College of Higher Education after the 1976 reorganisation.

BID FOR POLYTECHNIC STATUS

Harold Wilson commented in a speech to the Labour Party Conference at Scarborough in 1963 that *"our failure to develop science and technology is leading to a mass sellout to foreign concerns ... Great Britain, once the workshop of the world, is becoming the dumping ground for the products of overseas industries that are just that bit quicker at getting off the mark than we are"*.[17]

The perception of industry as not a career for 'high flyers' still remained a problem as was the assumption that boys only enter higher technical education when they could not get a place in the faculties of pure science. The Robbins Report of 1963 also pointed to the lack of females in higher technical education.

Fig. 32. Charterhouse Lane Annexe. (RB)

The Council for National Academic Awards (CNAA), formed as a result of the Robbins Report, started recognising degree level courses around 1965 and the College put forward seven of its courses for recognition, through the Yorkshire Council for Further Education. Unfortunately the YCFE rejected all but one of the courses in 1965 and an appeal to the Department of Education & Science a few months later proved unsuccessful although existing degree courses were allowed to continue. Before the CNAA was founded the College for many years was apparently the only one of its type in Yorkshire running degree courses. The Principal feared that the lack of recognition of the College's high level courses would lead to the better qualified staff leaving, the probable increased difficulty of staff recruitment and the impossibility of new courses emerging.

The White Paper, 'A Plan for Polytechnics and Other Colleges', was published in 1966. The Paper sought to be the solution of the problem of how to accommodate the demand for higher education in the further education system, "*Without prejudicing opportunities for the tens of thousands of less advanced students who wish to take courses at intermediate and lower levels*".[18] High level work was to concentrated in "a limited number of strong centres"[19] which would eventually mainly take students over eighteen pursuing full time, sandwich or part time courses leading to degrees or to qualifications just below degree level. A list of new Polytechnics was attached to the White Paper and did not include the Hull colleges.

As an initial response the Hull College of Technology urged the Secretary of State for Education & Science to consider the designation of the four Colleges for Further Education in Hull as a Polytechnic. The establishment of an Academic Board was also suggested as the present undemocrat-

Fig. 33. Crowle Street Annexe. (RS)

wildering" range of courses from hairdressing to degrees was inappropriate for a Polytechnic. The diverse range at Hull was due to a failure to build branch colleges after the county college ideas proposed in 1948 were abandoned.

A Times Educational Supplement supported the Government's rejection saying that the concentration of high level work in a small number of large organisations was necessary in terms of quality and economy and that the country's resources were already spread too thinly in this field. The White Paper suggested that 2000 full time students would be a minimum required for a Polytechnic; Hull only had 1500 full time students by 1970.

The Principal of the Hull College of Commerce, Mr Berry, also wrote an article for the Times Educational Supplement supporting the Polytechnic bid. He argued that concentration of high level work only made sense if a large amount of research work was to be done; this would not be the case in the new Polytechnics and the 2000 students figure was very arbitrary. Berry also thought that part time high level students would be hurt as they would have

ic Governing Board did not comply with the proposals in the White Paper. The bid for Polytechnic status was rejected by the DES, but in January 1967 the Secretary of State wrote to the Hull Authority stating that it *"would be prepared to review the question of establishing a Polytechnic in the Humberside area in the event of major developments resulting in substantial changes in the present position".*[20]

Hull Council's bid to have a Polytechnic received wide coverage in the educational press but none of it was complimentary. An article in 'Technical Education' commented on the Council's scheme: *"What is clear is that such encouragement is mischievous and irresponsible. If college lecturers are leaving Hull in droves (which is doubtful) the city can only blame its elected representatives and permanent officials who should have, and must have known better."*[21] The article also thought the "be-to travel large distances to study (Leeds was the nearest Polytechnic) and that good part time teachers would be lost. He also pointed out that Hull's high level work was a service to the local industries with mainly local students and such courses would be difficult to transfer.

Apart from the totally inadequate premises of the colleges of Commerce, Art and the Nautical College one of the main reasons Hull became the largest city without a Polytechnic was the relatively small amount of high level work carried on at the College of Technology. Just before and after the second world war a significant amount of degree work was done at the College but this did not develop. In 1966 there were only 641 students studying at HND or above level out of a total of 6325 but no degree course had double figures for any one year. *"The new College (of Technology) had failed to establish itself in the role of provider of viable full time high level courses."*[22]

The Hull College of Technology had some difficulty in retaining the levels and quality of work immediately after the Polytechnic scheme failed. The Departments of Physics and Mathematics were downgraded in 1968 from Burnham Grade III to Grade II. Mr H. Rose, Head of Physics, left the College in 1969 and the Physics and Mathematics Departments were combined with the Head of Mathematics, A. Longhorn, appointed Head of the new, Grade IV, department. Also in 1969 the Department of Engineering was downgraded from Grade V to Grade IV. By 1970 there does not appear to be any students studying for the London University External Degrees. Enrolment for the Engineering and the General BSc Degree ceased in 1968 and the HND Aeronautics and HND Mechanical were replaced by an HND Engineering course in September 1968. A five year part time BSc (London External) General Degree course had been proposed for September 1967. The course seemed to be aimed at teachers and was free to any Hull Teacher.

The Education Committee asked the Government to review Hull's case for Polytechnic Status in 1970; probably based on the imminent move of the other colleges (Art and Commerce) to Queen's Gardens. The Department of Education and Science remained unimpressed.

Plans for a new College of Commerce on the Queen's Gardens site were included in the 1963/64 building programme with the first phase of the new Art College included in the 1967/68 programme. Plans to move the Nautical College first appeared in 1964 and only a year later the Department of Education & Science approved the scheme. The College of Commerce and the Regional College of Art moved to the Queen's Gardens site by the early 1970s. The Nautical College rehoused to a site near Queens Gardens in 1974; most higher education colleges were finally on one central site. The communal block for the colleges was brought into use from October 1968.

Emlyn Jones retired in August 1970 to be replaced by Dr Reginald Herbert Rogers of Epsom.

THE COLLEGE OF FURTHER EDUCATION

The early 1970s saw a continued decline in high level work carried out at the Hull College of Technology and also a decline in total numbers from 6156 in 1969 to 5693 in 1973. In 1972 the Hull Education Committee suggested a new College of Further Education to house the low level work of the College of Technology, probably based on a statement in the 1972 Government White Paper, 'Education: a Framework for Expansion', that money would be available for buildings for the non-university higher education sector. However the Ministry rejected the scheme for 1974/75 and again the following year.

By 1972 it was clear that a new Humberside County Council would be created and that control of education would pass from Hull City Council to that new Authority. The City Council still had hopes of Polytechnic status and in 1972 recommended: "*That the Authority press the new Humberside County's claims for Polytechnic status with the Secretary of State for Education and Science.*"[23] Again in 1973 the Hull Education Committee announced: "*That the Humberside County Council be informed of the Council's aim to achieve Polytechnic status for Kingston Upon Hull as soon as possible, and of the Committee's intention to ask the County Coun-*

Fig. 34. Chapman Street Infant School closed in 1979 and became part of HCFE's Chapman Street Annexe. The extra classrooms were mainly used by the Department of Secretarial Studies. (RS)

cil to appoint representatives to join representatives of this Committee in meeting the Secretary of State for Education and Science to press this aim."[24] Humberside County Council took over from April 1974.

The 1972 White Paper also suggested that some colleges of education might develop jointly with other local colleges for further education. The Principals of the six Hull Colleges, Technology, Art, Commerce, Nautical, Education and the voluntary Endsleigh College of Education, met to discuss these proposals early in 1973 but could do nothing until representatives of Humberside County Council met the Governing Bodies of the colleges in May 1973. The colleges then had to chose between a loosely federated structure or a more tightly knit unitary structure with a strong central directorate (a Polytechnic) if they were to combine. Their

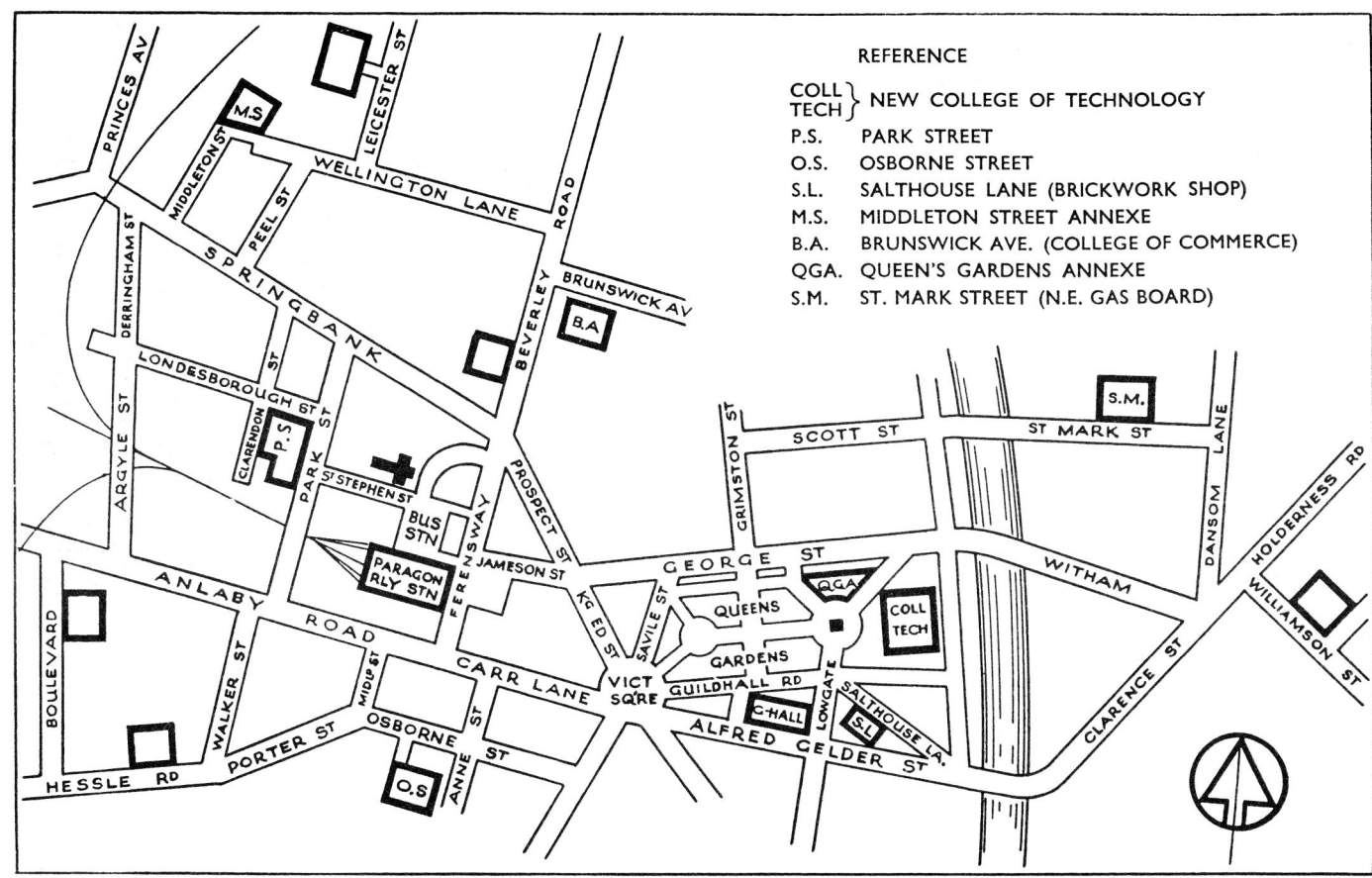

Fig. 35. College of Technology Annexes from 1965-66 Prospectus. (HC)

representatives decided to aim for a centralised college but this did not solve the problem of where to house the low level work; they decided it would be preferable to separate low level courses (roughly 'A' level and below) off into a College of Further Education. The decision would mean the end of the College of Technology as a 'straight through' institution incorporating courses from Hairdressing to HND's.

In January 1975 Humberside County Council proposed, after consulting the Governing Bodies of the colleges, that the six Hull colleges merge into a unitary institution of higher education with a single Governing Council, a single Academic Senate and several Faculty Boards. These new bodies were to be established using guidelines recommended in the DES Circular "The Development of Higher Education in the Non-Universities Sector".

Reorganisation took place in September 1976 and the six colleges formed Hull College of Higher Education and Hull College of Further Education (HCFE). The College of Higher Education later became Humberside College of Higher Education, then Humber-

*Fig. 36. **Thomas Stratten Annexe** closed in 1985/86 and the Special Educational Needs work transferred to Park Street.* (RS)

side Polytechnic and is now the University of Humberside. The College of Further Education was given responsibility for the provision and development of courses, generally speaking, up to GCE 'A' level standard.

Mr A. Tuck became Principal in January 1976, replacing Dr Rogers, to establish and develop the new College of Further Education; he was formerly Vice-Princi-

pal of Southall College of Technology.

The HCFE set-up an Academic Board, very similar to the old one, which was responsible to the Governing Body of the College; each academic department had a Board of Study which functioned as a sub-Committee of the Academic Board. New College Advisory Committees were set-up, which were responsible to the Governing Body, to link the College with industry and commerce. Also directly responsible to the Governing Body was the College Council that advised on the non-academic work of the College; it was the only body on which the whole College community was represented. A Joint Academic Liaison Committee was also set-up by the two Hull Colleges to advise the Academic Boards on matters of common interest to the colleges.

At reorganisation the College of Further Education still occupied a large number of annexes at:

> Chapman Street
> Charterhouse Lane
> Craven Street
> Crowle Street
> Courtney Street
> Middleton Street
> Park Street
> Salthouse Lane
> The Boulevard
> Thomas Stratten Annexe,

and in 1977 the College assumed responsibility for the Further Education work of the former Goole Further Education Centre.

RECENT ANNEXES AND THE INTRODUCTION OF YTS

The Departments of Construction and Engineering had been planning to rent industrial accommodation on Sutton Fields Estate so they could move out of the old, badly maintained annexes and provide courses for unemployed school leavers during 1979; however the Manpower Services Commission withdrew its financial support and the move never took place.

During the 1980/81 session HCFE leased an industrial unit on the Bankside Estate for Construction and Building workshops. The classrooms, machine/workshops and a canteen were built by members of staff partly during the summer vacation. Construction Industry Training Board (CITB) Courses in Carpentry and Joinery and Brickwork were transferred from the Thomas Stratten Annexe.

Also during 1980/81 the rationalisation between the colleges of higher and further education continued. The Humberside College of Higher Education's science and computer staff moved out of the main building at Queen's Gardens, with the exception of the Radioisotope suite; HCHE Marine Electronic classes ceased to use the gymnasium block at the Charterhouse Lane Annexe and the following year the radar installations and HCHE staff moved from the sixth floor at Queen's Gardens into the former Nautical College. The gymnasium block at Charterhouse Lane was converted into a special unit for educationally disadvantaged students by HCFE during 1981/82.

Hull College of Further Education acquired a large factory site in Ryde Avenue, Clough Road during 1981/82. It was hoped that accommodation at Park Street could be released to enable it to be used as a centre for the new Vocational Preparation courses for school leavers. The Co-op Garage and Warehouse on the Ryde Avenue site were purchased soon after. The Vocational Preparation Unit became established at Park Street in 1982/3. As a result of the Holland and Warnock Reports, extra provision for the education of young unemployed people between 16 and 19 and disadvantaged and disabled students had

Fig. 37. Malton Street Annexe. (RB)

been agreed to be implemented by HCFE from 1978.

A second Vice-Principal, Wendy Johnson-Brett, was appointed in April 1983 to oversee the development of the new Government Youth Training Scheme (YTS); the College had run pilot YTS courses, at Park Street, during the 1982/83 session and it seemed likely the College would become heavily involved in providing training places. The implementation of YTS for the August 1983 session was late and hurried with courses only starting at the end of September and the College received less funding than for the Youth Opportunities Programme the new courses replaced. In August a total embargo on full time posts at the College was imposed due to financial restriction by the County Council, this did not help the establishment of new courses.

The purpose of YTS was *"to provide young people with a better start in working and adult life through an integrated programme of training, education and work experience ... which can serve as a foundation for subsequent employment or continued training or relevant further education; to provide for the participating employer a better equipped young workforce; to develop and maintain a more versatile, readily adaptable, highly motivated and productive work force"*.[25]

The HE and FE Colleges 'swapped' some accommodation in 1982/83 with FE taking over the Malton Street School to develop trowel trade courses and HE taking over the brickwork shop in Salthouse Lane for its Art and Design Faculty. A new workshop block close to the main College was completed in 1984 and the CITB courses in Carpentry and Brickwork and Brickwork were transferred from Bankside in November 1985. The new Construction Workshop was officially opened on 19 February 1985 by Councillor V. Chapman, Chairman of Humberside County Council. HCHE and HCFE continued to swap courses and premises including some diploma courses transferring to HCFE; the Centre for International Studies and the former premises of the College of Commerce also became part of HCFE by 1989.

The main block at Queen's Gardens had to be repaired and reclad during 1982/3 causing severe disruption due to high noise levels. It was nearly Easter 1984 before the front doors of the building were finally able to be used again.

Hull College of Further Education closed the Crowle Street Annexe in 1984/85; the Electrical Engineering Services and Road Transport Studies sections were transferred to the Ryde Avenue Annexe. Welding, Shipbuilding and Fabrication courses were also transferred from Queen's Gardens, Thomas Stratten and Park Street to Ryde Avenue.

In October 1984 Humberside College of Higher Education agreed to move out of the workshop block at Queen's Gardens, with the exception of the Printing section. Unfortunately for HCFE they decided not to do ahead with the proposal but HCHE's Boulevard annexe and the Queen's Gardens Communal Block were transferred to HCFE. The following year three of the workshops were transferred from HCHE to HCFE. The Boulevard Annexe was mainly used for Business Studies and Catering courses by HCFE.

Sir Leo Schultz and Riley High Schools were taken over by HCFE in 1988 after they had been closed as secondary schools. Riley Centre,

Fig. 38. New CITB Workshop, Salthouse Lane, exterior. (RB)

as it was renamed, housed many of the Business Studies and Computing and Business Systems courses along with some of the Design courses and several Access and Community Education courses. Most of the Health and Community Care courses were run at Schultz as well as some Access and Community Education courses. Schultz was also the new base for the Outreach Project, run in partnership with Adult Education and the Careers Service. The Science sector also used a number of laboratories at the Schultz site. The Schultz Centre was vacated by the College in 1991.

Middleton Street Annexe was closed in 1989 and the Painting and Decorating courses moved to Charterhouse. Humberside County Council refurbished Middleton Street in 1990 as the Humberside Cultural Enterprise Centre and it became the base for Remould Theatre Company amongst other uses.

FURTHER REORGANISATION AND THE FUTURE

In his Annual report for 1981/82 the Principal, Mr Tuck, stated that,

Fig. 39. CITB Workshop interior, Salthouse Lane. (HC)

"The challenge facing this as all FE Colleges, namely the unique combination of demographic change, new technology and recession, must also be met on a College not departmental basis ... effective use of resources and pedagogical need dictates a change in organisational structure to meet the change of the 80s."[26]

During the year the number of part time students at the College was forecast to fall by 8% by the Government's Expenditure Steering Group as Hull had a higher unemployment rate than the national average but the attendance actually increased by 3% compared with 1980/81. The ESG also predicted a decrease in full time attendance of 9% but the number of students rose by 29% and evening attendance increased by 12%.

During the 1978/79 session the number of students at HCFE had passed the 10,000 mark for the first time with 9000 of them attending part time. The following year the number of students decreased by 1000 due to restrictions on manpower and finances imposed on the College; a number of classes were not held and others ran with re-duced hours although the College did save £77,830 between 1 September 1979 and 31 March 1980.

The 1985/86 session saw severe financial restraints with some courses not run and a reduction in staff. The budget to the College was cut from 1984/85 to 1986/87 and additional savings had to be made on top of the cuts.

Mr Tuck retired in 1986 to be replaced by Graham Worthington as Principal of Hull College of Further Education.

In the past liaison with local schools and industry had often been dependant upon individual initiatives by members of staff. This situation was improved by the introduction of a College Marketing Unit in 1988/89 which centrally co-ordinated links with other organisations.

The HM Inspectors Report of autumn 1989 was mixed but on the whole very favourable to the College. It pointed to inadequate capital investments but, *"There are many strengths, including good examination results, good prospects for employment or higher education, excellent induction and tutorial arrangements, and course evaluation procedures which are searching and thorough.*

The College has gone through a time of rapid change and reorganisation in virtually every area of its provision. The management structures, at all levels, appear well-designed and able to constitute a firm framework on which the College can build and consolidate.

It is already well on its way to achieving its stated aim of providing a good quality education and training experience for all of its students."[27]

The College experienced quite severe financial difficulties during the period 1989-1991 as it coped within funding arrangements which did not fully reflect the need for building improvements and course expansion. Peter Moseley, previously Principal at South Nottingham College, was appointed Principal in May 1992, just as the Government determined to establish further education colleges as independent charitable corporations.

Under the 1992 Further and Higher Education Act the College became independent of Local Authority (Humberside County Council) control on 1 April 1993 for the first time since the Municipal Technical School started in 1893. The College shortened its name to just Hull College and adopted Wilberforce monument as a logo. Funding now came from the Further Education Funding Council rather than the Local Education Authority. Dr Stubbs, of the F.E.F.C. presented the prizes at a Centenary Awards Ceremony at Hull City Hall on 14 October 1993. At the Awards Ceremony Mr Moseley said that one of the main reasons for the Government making Colleges independent was that they should become more efficient and business-like. "It is right that we should be efficient, but we are not a business - it is not our job to make a profit, it is our job to provide a high quality public education service for all sections of the community but in a proper business-like manner, using the public's money in a sensible and effective way. Using our funds for the benefit of local children and families."

Under the new system of funding there may be less formal democratic accountability, but the College Governors are still local councillors and business people. The new Governing Body publically recognised the importance of extending local links. It is determined to provide a quality of educational service to the community which helps the economic and social development of Hull and its people.

Under the new funding arrangements, the College is responsible for its own financial destiny. The national government over a four year period reduced the level of funding available for each student by almost twenty percent. By increasing the student numbers considerably, however, the College was able to secure additional resources and was able to begin to tackle the problems of bringing the buildings up to a reasonable state of repair. Major refurbishments have been completed at the Queen's Gardens and Park Street Centres. The financial problems of the late 1980s were overcome through the contribution and flexibility of staff and the extension of the College's services.

As the College approaches the millennium, it is looking forward to re-establishing close relations with Hull City Council and its new Education Department. Kingston upon Hull recognises the importance of extending educational opportunities to young people and adults, if it is to secure the economic development necessary to safeguard the future for the region. Partners, drawn from the Universities, the Schools, the Voluntary Sector and businesses, have joined together to promote City Learning in order to work collaboratively to help Kingston upon Hull become one of the great Learning Cities. Hull College is proud, once more, to be at the heart of the City's development.

Notes for Chapter Three

1. Ministry of Education, Higher Technological Education, HMSO, 1945 (The Percy Report).

2. Hull Corporation, Scheme of Further Education & Plan for County Collages, 1948.

3. Minutes of Hull Education Committee, 1 May 1953.

4. Ibid., 19 August 1946.

5. Hull Daily Mail, 4 December 1956.

6. P. Venables, Technical Education: Its Aims, Organisation and Future Development, G. Bell & Sons, 1955.

7. Ministry of Education, Technical Education, February 1956.

8. Ministry of Education Circular 305: The Organisation of Technical Colleges, 1956.

9. R. H. Mitchell, The Development Of Hull College of Technology, 1975. (University of Hull Thesis. I would like to thank the University for permission to quote from this work.)

10. Ibid.

11. Ibid.

12. Ministry of Education Circular 98: The Status of Technical, Commercial and Art Colleges, 1946.

13. Ibid.

14. R. H. Mitchell, 1975.

15. Hull Daily Mail, 15 May 1962.

16. Ibid., C1963.

17. G. Roderick & M. Stephens, The British Malaise, Falmer Press, 1982.

18. Dept. of Education & Science Circular, Technical College Resources: Size of Classes and Approval of Further Education Courses, 1966.

19. Ibid.

20. Minutes of H.E.C., 14 April 1967.

21. Technical Education & Industrial Training, Vol. 9, July 1967.

22. R. H. Mitchell, 1975.

23. Minutes of H.E.C., 17 April 1972.

24. Ibid., 7 May 1973.

25. Newsletter, Hull College of Further Education, July 1983.

26. Principal's Annual Report, H.C.F.E., 1982.

27. The Magazine, H.C.F.E., Autumn 1989.

THE FIRST REPORT

Dr. Riley made his first report on the School for the year ending 31 August 1895 when there had been a total of 889 day and evening students. In general he thought that the first full year had been very successful although there were still some problems. The Engineering Laboratory had not yet been fully furnished, limiting the amount of practical work that could be done. Attendance for plumbing, milling, building construction, carpentry and sanitary science had been disappointing, mainly due to poor accommodation and not enough practical work. Marine Engineering classes suffered from students having to go to sea or leave to seek employment elsewhere. The Commercial and Women's classes had been very well attended and advanced students of the Commercial Department took examinations of the Royal Society of Arts or Sir Isaac Pitman & Son's Certificates.

CHANGES IN STAFF AND CLASSES

There were inevitably some important staff changes during the first years, G. Carr Robinson had been allowed to earn some private money from his chemistry practice if this did not conflict with his college duties. He complained that the college took all his time and asked for an increased salary but the Committee refused and offered him a full time post as Teacher of Chemistry. Robinson declined the offer and left the college in 1895 to be replaced by Harry Ingle PhD. Dr Ingle only stayed a year, leaving to become a research chemist in Scotland. Dr Ingle's replacement was A. C. Wright MA, assistant lecturer at Yorkshire College, Leeds. The Chief Engineering Lecturer, R. Durley, left in 1896 to take the post of Assistant Professor of Mechanical Engineering at Mc Gill University, Montreal. The Committee commended Durley for his work at the school. Mons O Baumann was replaced by C. Kessler MA and the Student Assistant in the Chemistry Department was appointed chemist in a Sheffield Steel Works.

The Chemistry lecturer, A. C. Wright, resigned in 1897 to become a chemist with Blundell & Spence. He was replaced by Thomas Luxton who had been chemistry teacher at the Higher Grade Central School in Brunswick Avenue. The Assistant Lecturer on Engineering resigned in 1901 he was replaced by Hector Garrett a draughtsman at Earle's and a former student at the Technical School.

Brickwork and Masonry classes had to be withdrawn in 1896 due to the poor accommodation. Three students were prohibited from sitting the examination in Mechanical Construction and charged with insubordination in the same year for complaining that the accommodation at the examination was inadequate.

At the end of the academic year, 31 August 1896, there had been a total of 375 students in the day department and 1235 in the evening classes, this compared with 247 and 876 the previous year.

For the day classes this broke down to:

	1896	1895
Junior Engineering	31	29
Senior Engineering	35	5
Chemistry	7	11
Commercial	27	11
Special Courses	5	-
Women's Industries	270	191

The proportion of women studying seems rather large but they usually had more time during the day to attend classes than men. Many employers were very reluctant to give men time off during the day to attend the Technical School. Hull offered few opportunities for women's work, outside the cotton mills that closed down in 1894 and some of the fish trades.

The quality of work in the Commercial Department was very high compared with the other 196 centres in the country taking Society of Arts Examinations:

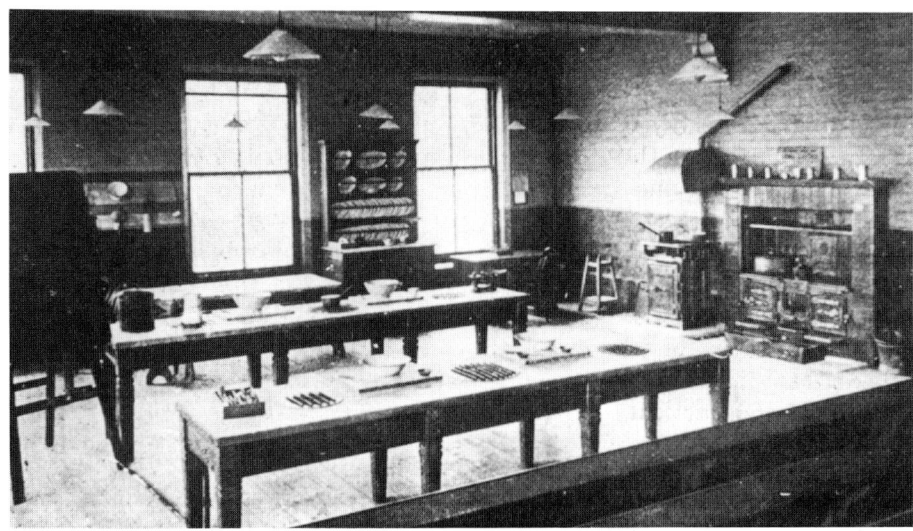

Fig. 40. Kitchen Workshop, 1900 (HC)

	Firsts	Seconds	Thirds	Failures
HMTS	21.57%	37.25%	37.25%	3.93%
Rest	11.32%	31.42%	38.12%	19.14%

Dishes made in cookery classes were sold to students at a little over cost price. The profit was used to cover the cost of soap, starch, etc. in the laundry department. In the Women's Department dinners were provided for the students at 3½d and 4d by 1899. By 1902 profits from cookery products went to the Boy's Sports Fund and for prizes in the Cookery and Laundry Departments. Miss Freeborough who had been responsible for the success of the cookery and laundry classes left after 8 years at the College in 1902.

There was an increasing demand for University and professional examinations and some students were already studying Matriculation, Intermediate Arts, Intermediate Science, Preliminary Science and First Bachelor of Science Examinations of the London University (Intermediate corresponds roughly to an 'A' level today). Riley suggested that University preparation courses should be available in the evening as well as the day classes. The first degrees awarded for work done in the School came in 1898, a Bachelor of Laws and a Bachelor of Science from London University and a Bachelor of Science from Durham University.

In his end of year report for 1897 Riley was pleased that more advanced engineering work was now being done and that attendance generally had improved. There were still no examinations in the Women's Industries Department, apart from Dressmaking, due to a lack of accommodation. There were a total of 416 day and 1552 evening students.

The Art School had large classes for a provincial school with 110 day and 112 evening students. Some students of the Art School had also been sitting examinations in art at the Technical College, this was discontinued after 1897 as the Art

School complained about the loss of revenue.

Some new classes took place at the request of industry during 1898, 70 students started a typography course and there were 22 requests to start ambulance classes. Some classes were over full and had to be limited to Hull residents only.

By 1898 there were 483 day and 1962 evening students and in the following year this had increased to 152 in the Day and Technical Department with 492 in cookery classes and 2098 evening students.

Riley commented that a great obstacle to doing advanced work was the short time students had spent in elementary school and he suggested that the entry age to the Technical School should be raised. Most classes had been well attended although the engineering classes were badly affected by the engineers' strike.

Most classes had transferred to Park Street by 1899 except the Fishermen's School that moved to Harrow Street. Plumbing students moved from George Street in September 1898 but it was a further

two years before the Chemistry Department could transfer fully from Bond Street.

Parish and Berry were commissioned to take a series of external and internal photographs for the first illustrated prospectus in 1900. Most of the rooms can still be recognised: the Wood Workshop is Room 25 (G25); the Plumbing Workshop is Rooms 4 & 5 (G5 & 6); the Electrical Engineering Laboratory is Room 24 (G24); the Elementary Electrical Laboratory is Room 21 (G21); and the Examinations Hall is now the Library.

Home study by 1900 had appreciably diminished in consequence of the large amount of time devoted to studying the Boer War news, according to Riley. Six students went to the front, two in the Imperial Yeomanry and the rest as ambulance men and telegraphists. Unfortunately, students were still doing very little homework by 1902 and a note in the prospectus stated that pupils must do homework or they could be suspended from their course.

A new course of preliminary instruction for plumbers started during 1900, hopefully this could give the students the necessary background to progress to the advanced classes in Sanitary Plumbing. For

Fig. 41. Electrical Engineering Laboratory (HC)

Fig. 42. Physics Lecture Theatre
(HC)

*Fig. 43. Elementary
Chemistry Laboratory,
1900* (HC)

Fig. 44. Elementary Electrical Laboratory (HC)

Fig. 45. The Examination Hall, 1900 (HC)

1900 there was at total of 709 day and 2464 evening students.

Overall the College did well and in 1902 out of 325 centres in the country taking City & Guilds Hull came fourth for medals gained. Riley was still surprised at the lack of encouragement given to mechanical and civil engineering students by employers; he pointed out that 60% of men in responsible positions in American firms were recruited through technological colleges.

INCREASED COURSES

From 1903 Junior School pupils were allowed to be apprentices at the School with the agreement of Rose, Down & Thompson, a major engineering firm in Hull. This very liberal move meant that time spent at the school would count towards the pupil's apprenticeship.

The Technical School had a good year for exam results in 1903 and in the whole country only four students were called to London to take the exam in Honours Part 2 Electricity two of whom were from the Hull School. Typography and breadmaking classes suffered from a lack of practical classes and it was decided, in principle, to build new workshops although these would have to be in a new building. Unfortunately better facilities for these classes were not provided until the early 1930s.

The range of courses on offer at technical schools widened after 1904 when the Board of Education gave grants for subjects other than those approved by the Science and Art Department. This, it was hoped, would attract better teachers who could devise their own courses. Riley thought one of the greatest deficiencies of technical education was in the supply of student teachers from the training colleges. The training colleges could supply 2800 teachers annually but over 5000 trained teachers were required to meet the growing demand.

For the first year since reorganisation (1903-04) the Government Inspectors reports were quite favourable, in the Junior Section *"good systematic work is being done in science, mathematics and the teaching reaches a high standard. The organisation of the school is excellent."*[1] For the Senior Section *"the school is very well conducted; but the curriculum may need revision when more experience has been gained. At present hardly sufficient time seems to be devoted to mathematics either in the Engineering or the Chemical Departments. In the first year Engineering Course the amount of time devoted to practical work in the laboratories is perhaps inadequate - no use is made of the mechanical laboratory."*[2]

Reports on the evening classes of the School were equally encouraging. *"The organisation and management of these classes are excellent, as are also the teaching and the work done there.*

Progress in connection with the Institution (the Technical School) is possible by co-ordinating the work done in it with that in the other Evening Schools in Hull. Portions of the elementary work at the Technical School and some of the classes unconnected with any of the chief courses might with advantage be transferred to the YPI and the Boulevard, Central and Craven Street Schools. It might be pointed out that at the latter schools there are good classrooms and laboratories of which practically no use is made in the evening. In this way the Technical School will have room, as its numbers increase, for the special and more advanced work for which it is excellently equipped."[3]

T H Wilson, Sons & Co., ship owners, shipping and insurance agents, suggested a scheme of instruction for their clerks in 1906 involving a four year course at the Technical

School; all new clerks would have to take the course. As a result of this progressive move an Evening School of Commerce was formed and W. H. C. Jukes appointed as teacher of commercial subjects.

By 1907 the prospectus had become rather large and for the first time it was issued in two parts, one for evening classes and the other for day classes.

The Hull Jeweller's Association was established in 1908 and one of its first concerns was to train apprentices. The Technical School agreed to set-up classes in theoretical and practical work. In the same year the typographical classes expanded to include practical printing; the equipment cost £550 and was installed in Room 31 (F3). There were around 100 apprentices in the printing industry, half of these were in newspapers and could not benefit from the course, but only 40 pupils were needed for the classes to be successful.

DEVELOPMENTS AT THE TECHNICAL SCHOOL, 1910s

The English Master left the School to be replaced by E. Percy Bates from January 1904. In the same year the Government Inspectors gave a favourable report and requested photographs of the School for the Board of Education at South Kensington. In 1910 Bates was awarded an MA of London University in the branch of Medieval and Modern Languages, after examination and the submission of a thesis on 'Loan Words in Gothic' and a subsidiary thesis on 'English Satirists.'

The School decided that a reference and lending library was essential as neither the public nor subscription libraries stocked the necessary books and began to set one up in 1908 partly with profits from the cookery classes. There was a serious fire in the same year causing £103 damage to the roof above the staircase.

Junior technical education became recognised as a separate form of instruction by the Board of Education in 1913. Hull's Junior Day School was quite unique in that courses were for four years rather than the normal two or three and it was hoped that pupils would progress to the Technical College courses. The Board would unfortunately only recognise three year courses and gave the College until 1916 to reorganise. The College extended the senior courses by starting a new general one year course to act as a buffer between the Junior Day School and the Day Technical Insti-

tute. The new first year course attracted 37 students when run for the first time in 1916. Physical education also became part of the curriculum for the first time in the Junior School.

In September 1910 the name 'Hull Municipal Technical College' replaced the existing 'School' sign above the entrance at Park Street. A scheme for awarding internal College Diplomas and Certificates started in 1910 and had developed by 1912. There was a Diploma exam for students of at least two years standing in the Senior Day Departments and a School Leaving Certificate for boys of at least three years standing in the Junior Day Departments. In the evening schools there were single subject exams in every subject and stage taught.

Luxton regretted that advanced students continued to be lost as they almost invariably left after the apprenticeship was complete. The large amount of overtime work available to men over 18 was also a disincentive to continue studying.

In 1911 the Board of Education discontinued the lower grade Science and Art examinations and in 1918 the advanced examinations, together with the lower examinations of the City and Guilds, were abol-

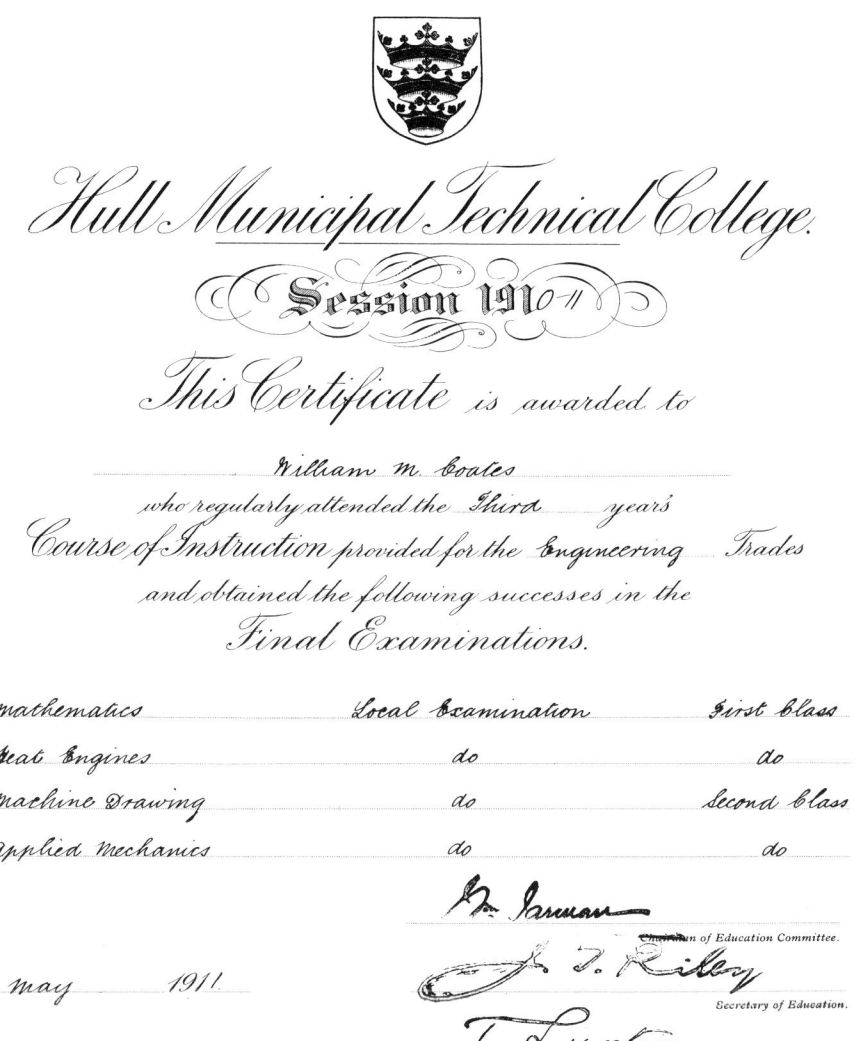

Fig. 46. Hull Municipal Technical College Certificate

ished. These moves resulted in the establishment of regional examination boards. The number of students taking external examinations had gradually been declining and The Yorkshire Board of Examinations was formed in 1914 to help combat this; certificates were mutually recognised by the schools awarding them. An attempt was made to introduce non vocational evening classes in literature, music, etc. at the College but the results were not very encouraging.

THE FIRST WORLD WAR

The military fully occupied some rooms in the College and partially used others along with the south yard from December 1914. By March 1915 the military occupation had ended apart from two rooms that were still used for administrative purposes by the 11th and 13th Hull Services Battalions and the 2nd Hull Volunteer Battalion. Classes in French and German, lasting 20 weeks, were organised for officers and non commissioned officers with classes in camp cookery for the private soldiers. Additional instruction classes for farriers, shoeing smiths, saddlers and telephonists were also provided at the request of the military.

Technical staff of the Humber Defences were also installed in Park Street with their workmen in the workshops and the largest lathe at the College was loaned to a local munitions factory.

Just before the war started a comprehensive scheme of instruction in mechanical and electrical engineering and shipbuilding on the 'sandwich system' had been arranged and accepted by the leading employers of the City, unfortunately the war prevented its implementation.

In an attempt to raise the numbers in the Day Technical Institute the scholarship system had to be altered from 1917. The existing six scholarships were to be replaced by a sandwich system with twenty scholarships awarded to apprentices in the engineering trade with a further ten scholarships for new advanced courses.

In 1916 boilermakers at Earl's Shipbuilding stressed on their apprentices the need to attend College courses and advanced them the cost of fees, books and materials, to be repaid later. As a result of this very progressive action 35 boilermakers attended classes in Craven Street.

Courses of specialised training in commercial subjects were offered to women willing to replace male clerks who joined the Forces. However, the College did not think that running engineering courses for women would be worthwhile. Immediately after the War there was a remarkable increase in women attending general evening classes. In the Women's Institutes themselves the removal of a rigid course system immediately led to an increase in numbers from 392 in 1917/18 to 757 in 1918/19.

During the War evening classes were severely disrupted by the frequent Zeppelin alarms, dark streets and the great slump in building and allied trades. The Senior Chemistry Department had to close as all its students were in the Army. Twelve members of staff were on active service in 1916.

Late in 1916 wounded soldiers were encouraged to take industrial training as therapy rather than having a long period of convalescence, all fees were to be free. It had not been possible to provide disabled and demobilised soldiers with as many training places as hoped but full time courses were set up in 1918/19 in watch and clock making and accountancy and business training. Some ex-soldiers joined the usual college course and had their fees and expenses paid for by the Government.

The business training courses were very successful with a total of 82 students in three classes. Two extra members of staff had to be recruited to cope with running the usual courses in the Day School. Some 24 men passed the exams for the Association of the Chartered Institute of Secretaries and a large number of other successes in the advanced stages of the Royal Society of Arts were obtained. With the exception of three or four all the ex-servicemen taking the business training courses gained good employment. The training courses ran for two years.

A rigid age limit of 12½ - 13½ for entry to the Junior Day School was imposed by the Board of Education for the 1916/17 session for the first time. Luxton thought this had a disastrous effect on the boys and the College; large numbers of able students had to be turned away effectively ending their day school education at 14. The organic link between the Junior School and the Senior Department had been broken, removing the only adequate supply of well-trained boys for the senior school. On the positive side a Free Admission Card Scheme produced a good supply of well-trained boys and girls for the Evening Schools. The scheme offered free admission to evening classes as a reward for an excellent day school record. The following year 1622 pupils were offered free places and 55.8% of them accepted.

Accommodation problems became acute in 1917 as all branch commercial schools, except Villa Place, were quite full, the three branch technical schools were full to overflowing and the Central School of Commerce was full four nights a week. Two additional branch commercial schools opened in the 1918/19 session one ran by the Hull Unity Club and a new school in Beverley Road opened in co-operation with Needler's Ltd. for their employees.

As an alternative for *"boys who did not take kindly to compulsory football"*[4] a gardening scheme was proposed in 1918 to provide them with fresh air. Part of the playing fields on Cottingham Road were used to grow foodstuffs during the War but it was hoped that after they would be purely decorative and that sympathetic, semi-scientific training in the principles of gardening would be given.

The College purchased four aircraft engines from the Aircraft Salvage Department of the Government in 1919 for £5. They were a Rotary Gnome - 80 HP, RAF - 140 HP (air cooled), Renault 75 HP (air cooled) and an RAF 200 HP (water cooled).

The traditional view that technical institutes should only teach theoretical, not practical, skills began to break down after the First World War. This led to the establishment of Major and Minor courses; Minor courses taught workshop skills while Major courses taught theory. Course content inevitably often overlapped.

NATIONAL CERTIFICATES

The welcome move to national certification came in 1921 when the Institute of Mechanical Engineers developed a scheme to issue national certificates and diplomas in mechanical engineering. The success of this scheme led to the introduction of similar certificates, for example Chemistry (1921), Electrical Engineering (1923), Naval Architecture (1926), Building (1929), Textiles (1934), Civil Engineering (1943), Applied Physics, Metallurgy (1945) and Applied Chemistry (1947).

The certificates are of two levels. The Ordinary National Certificate is awarded after a senior part time course of three years and the Higher National Certificate after an advanced part time course of two years for those who have passed the ONC. Ordinary and Higher National Diplomas became available to full time students in technical colleges. The technical college drew up its own syllabus and submitted it to the Board of Education and the relevant professional institution. The scheme had many advantages, students gained a qualification approximate to a university degree and the standard of teaching rose considerably.

Luxton welcomed the new certificates as a fitting crown to the extensive scheme of local examinations and that at last there would be a national diploma or certificate of real value for advanced students. In 1930/31 six students complied with the conditions at the end of the first course at the Technical College for full time Diploma of the Institute of Mechanical Engineers.

DEVELOPMENTS AT THE TECHNICAL COLLEGE 1920s, 1930s

To help the overcrowding at the Technical College the Hall was divided into three rooms and room 63a (S3) divided in two, by glass partitions, in 1920.

The senior Chemistry Department could now provide full time degree courses. Luxton pointed to the fact that while many old boys of the chemistry department had secured high academic distinction, only one had ever secured satisfactory permanent employment in Hull. He also commented that there was little chance of employment locally for any boy over 18 in mechanical engineering. If the engineering industry continued not to value well trained men for their lower supervisory posts the full time engineering department of the College could perish.

The 1921/22 session attracted BSc Chemistry students from Kingswood, Ackworth, Sedbergh and Heywood but only three from local secondary schools.

Fig. 47. Senior Chemistry Laboratory (HC)

By November 1921 the Senior Engineering Department was in crisis with only 20 students and little prospect of numbers increasing; the fall was mainly due to ex-servicemen leaving the course. Unfortunately none of the ex-servicemen had obtained reasonable employment and many 5th, 6th and 7th year evening engineering students were also without work. To avoid sacking most of the engineering staff and to show that the College was still interested in its former pupils Luxton proposed a course for unemployed engineers and chemists, under 21, at reduced cost.

For 1921 a charge of 3d was made for the Technical College and Central School of Commerce evening prospectuses with the exception of 500 Technical and 250 Commercial complimentary copies. An 8 page pamphlet giving general information replaced the 4 page pamphlets used by the Branch Schools and the Women's Industries. The Junior School prospectus had not been printed since 1918 and the Senior Department prospectus since 1915. Five hundred Junior and 200 Senior prospectuses were printed in 1921. Charging for the prospectus proved to be a failure as fewer than 50% were disposed of and the experiment was not repeated. The Students Guide to Evening Classes was not reprinted.

A survey was conducted by the Association of Principals in Technical Institutions showing the cost and volume of work of 26 of the largest Technical Colleges in England and Wales for the 1921/22 session. Hull was fourth for total student hours but gross average expenditure per 100 student hours, the average expenditure on salaries per 100 student hours and the average expenditure on salaries per class hour were all less than in any other of the 26 institutions. The volume of work for the 1922/23 session would have placed Hull in second place.

There was an economy campaign in 1922/23 this had a disastrous effect with reduced numbers of classes and larger class sizes. Summer evening classes were also abandoned for the year. The number of staff at the Technical College and its affiliated schools exceeded 300 in 1922. A sandwich system was introduced for apprentices between 18 and 21 in the Day Engineering Department for the 1923/24 session. No fee was to be charged for the course. It was also proposed to re-equip the Engineering Department, in stages, at a cost of £850.

In 1923 the College applied to the Board of Education for recognition as a school for training marine engineers. The scheme involved full time training for boys between 15 and 18 followed by a full three years apprenticeship in an engineering workshop. John Quine was appointed Chief Instructor at the Adult Marine Engineering School in March 1924 and the school opened in the April. Unfortunately correspondence courses had to be set-up in marine engineering in

1924/25 because of the low numbers on the Technical College course.

In 1923/24 for the first year since the War there was no problem placing pupils in employment from the Day Departments. Encouragingly a number of employers now only took boys over 16.

The Technical College was full in the evenings and 41 classes had to be transferred to Wawne Street School in 1926, under the charge of R. A. Brown. This was only partially successful as the students still had to come back to Park Street for practical work. The Domestic Science Department at Park Street was closed and the students transferred to a new Centre at Day Street School and the Brunswick Avenue Central School. An additional branch technical school opened at Middleton Street making six in total.

Also in 1926 classes for policemen in proficiency were suggested to be held at Wawne Street School and paid for by the Watch Committee and the Home Office. However, these had to be abandoned as there were no funds for rental, however, 150 Sergeants and policemen said they were willing to pay the full rate for classes at the Central Police Station.

The Senior Departments of the College began to suffer by 1928 with the inevitable extinction of the university class (as Hull University College had been founded) although more short part time courses were set-up to compensate. Mr Gibson, head of engineering, was appointed Principal of Dudley Technical College, the ninth member of staff to obtain the rank of Principal of a Technical College.

Bates gave his thoughts on the lack of part time day classes in his 1928 report. *"Apart from their direct value to productive industry and the steadying influence on the growing youth of the country, continuative education has the merit of being far and away the cheapest form of educational activity. On these grounds as well as others, I feel justified in pleading for a wider outlook on the problem than that which exists at present. There is urgent need for more part time day courses to relieve some of the fatigue on growing boys and girls, who often work harder than their adult critics. Day time classes for technical instruction are especially necessary for girls who mean to earn their livelihood in the drapery establishments, shops, factories and warehouses. Technical training for life is just as valuable to the girl as to the boy, and at present such training in Hull is practically non-existent."* ... *"Continuative education ought therefore to visualise three things as essentials, part time technical courses by agreement with employers, a great extension of the facilities for rational social intercourse, and a share in the local provision for physical and especially outdoor recreation."*[5]

During the 1928/29 session a number of companies including the London & North Eastern Railway and associations like the Master Printers started to 'liberate' their apprentices for daytime study. During the day there had been 128 apprentices at the college during work time.

The Hairdressers' Society needed co-operation from the Education Committee to train their apprentices and the Committee rented the premises of the Oderma Toilet Saloon Co., Spring Bank, as they had the necessary specialist equipment, in September 1929. The classes were full to overflowing in the first year.

The Engineering Laboratory was remodelled in 1929 and wired for A. C. work at a cost of £2000. The printing department was given a rotary offset lithographic machine, a lithographic press and a Monotype machine with twin keyboards, caster and display attachment. The Master Butchers' Federation gave

£250 for a complete shop at the college for practical work including a Frigidaire and a Hobart electric sausage machine.

A school for wireless operators was approved at the end of 1929 and opened in September 1930 with 25 students and the following year attracted 88 students. Sawmilling classes started at 20 Chapel Lane from July 1930.

The Technical College was re-equipped at a cost of £827 in 1930. The work lasted most of the year causing severe disruption to day

classes. The following year the former boiler building was converted into a testing laboratory equipped with a new Avery Testing Machine. Bates commented that electrical engineering was rapidly overhauling the mechanical engineering classes and that the type of boy who enters it is rather better than in the older industry. All day department classes saw an increase in numbers during 1930/31 due to a recognition that students needed to obtain some definite diploma in order to secure employment at the end of the course.

Fig. 48. The Old Testing Laboratory (HC)

An experimental course for farmers in 1930/31 proved very successful attracting 32 farmers from every part of Holderness and taught soil chemistry, agriculture and agricultural botany. These courses were the first of their kind to be run in Yorkshire and were in co-operation with the University of Leeds and The East Riding Authority although the East Riding only provided support for a year. The course was extended to two years the following year and three years the year after and a diploma was awarded to the successful students.

The classes in oilmilling were praised by the City and Guilds in 1932 and they urged other cities to follow Hull's example. In 1934/35 the two year course in oilmilling attracted 136 students of whom 115 attended the first year course - the largest single class ever held at the Technical College at the time.

The National Economy (Education) Order, 1931 placed further expenditure restrictions on the Hull Education Committee. The restrictions made the instigation of anything new at the Technical College difficult.

A course on Television was planned for 1931/32 with the Northern Area representative of the Television Society, Mr Wolfson, of Leeds, as lec-turer. It is not clear if this course ever started.

Classes for bakers and confectioners did start in 1933 in the Bakery of the National Kitchens, 30 Hessle Road, with 34 students in the first year. A School for trawler engineers and trimmers started in 1934 at 32 Hessle Road. The course was free and arranged in agreement with Hull Steam Fishing Vessel Owners' Association, the School moved to St Andrew's Dock almost immediately.

The Productive Engineering course was reorganised to cover the National Certificate in 1934. An improvement in local industry led to a 10% increase in attendance at the Technical College during 1934/35. The following year, however, Bates commented that there was still a prejudice against engineering and a consequent low recruitment of good Secondary and Central school boys.

The attitude of the building trades employers greatly improved during 1933/34 and the Federation of Master Builders approved a scheme for part time day courses. Approximately 30 apprentices were liberated for one or two half days per week. The Blackburn Aircraft Co. liberated a number of students for one afternoon per week in 1933.

Part time courses existed at the College to enable students in full time attendance at other institutions to take up scientific courses that would otherwise be out of their reach. In 1936/37 Students were received from the College of Commerce, High School for Girls, Boulevard Nautical School, Withernsea Central School, Trinity House and others.

By the 1940s-50s the one year Inter. BSc in Science course also had students from grammar schools such as Newland High, St Mary's, Bridlington Girls High, because science and mathematics teachers were not available in those schools at the time. This connection lasted into the 1960s. Evolving from these courses came the GCE 'A' level programme which for a time ran as a two year course but had to be reduced to one year 'refresher' courses. Following deregulation Hull College now competes with sixth form colleges and again offers full two year 'A' level courses.

New Regulations extinguished the evening Pharmacy classes after 1936/37 although they continued as full time classes. A new pre-nursing course attracted nine girls in 1938/39. Girls could not take the usual nursing course until they were 17 and needed preliminary classes; the pre-nursing course pro-

Fig. 49. The Original wind tunnel, probably at 32 Hessle Road (HC)

vided a route to a degree level qualification.

During 1938/39 the evening classes for Women's Work were moved out of the College due to a lack of space.

Bates thought the reluctance of employers to release students during the day was short sighted and in 1938 he thoroughly condemned evening classes. *"They lacked continuity, were expensive, had no control over the students and were slow in producing the product. Part time day classes were far better and should be adopted by industry."*[6]

AERONAUTICS, A UNIQUE DEVELOPMENT

In July 1930 Hull University College suggested that a Diploma in Aeronautics should be organised with the co-operation of the Technical College; this was approved and the first students arrived in 1934 after spending two years in industry. The course work was shared equally between the University and the Technical College but none of the applied science or engineering work ever transferred to the University; premises in Hessle Road were probably used as a base for the Technical College work. The Aeronautics course was extended to two years in 1935/36. Seven stu-

Fig. 50. Aeronautical Engineering Department c1945/46
Front Row: Iddon, Howland, Greaves, Wheatley, Johnson
Back Row: Howard, Barber, Barnard, Bellerby (HC)

dents attended the two year course in 1936/37 and this had risen to 23 by 1943/44. Some specialist equipment had to be acquired, including a wind tunnel with a four foot section donated by the Westland Aircraft Company and its four bladed propeller was said to have come from the R100 or 101 airship. The Technical College also collaborated with the University on a course for handicraft teachers and with the

Nautical School on a course in marine biology in 1934.

In April 1943 the Elementary Education Subcommittee of Hull City Council transferred Middleton Street School to the Higher Education Subcommittee to be used for Aeronautical Training. The Ministry of Education approved of the plan and the cost of equipment and alterations were estimated to be

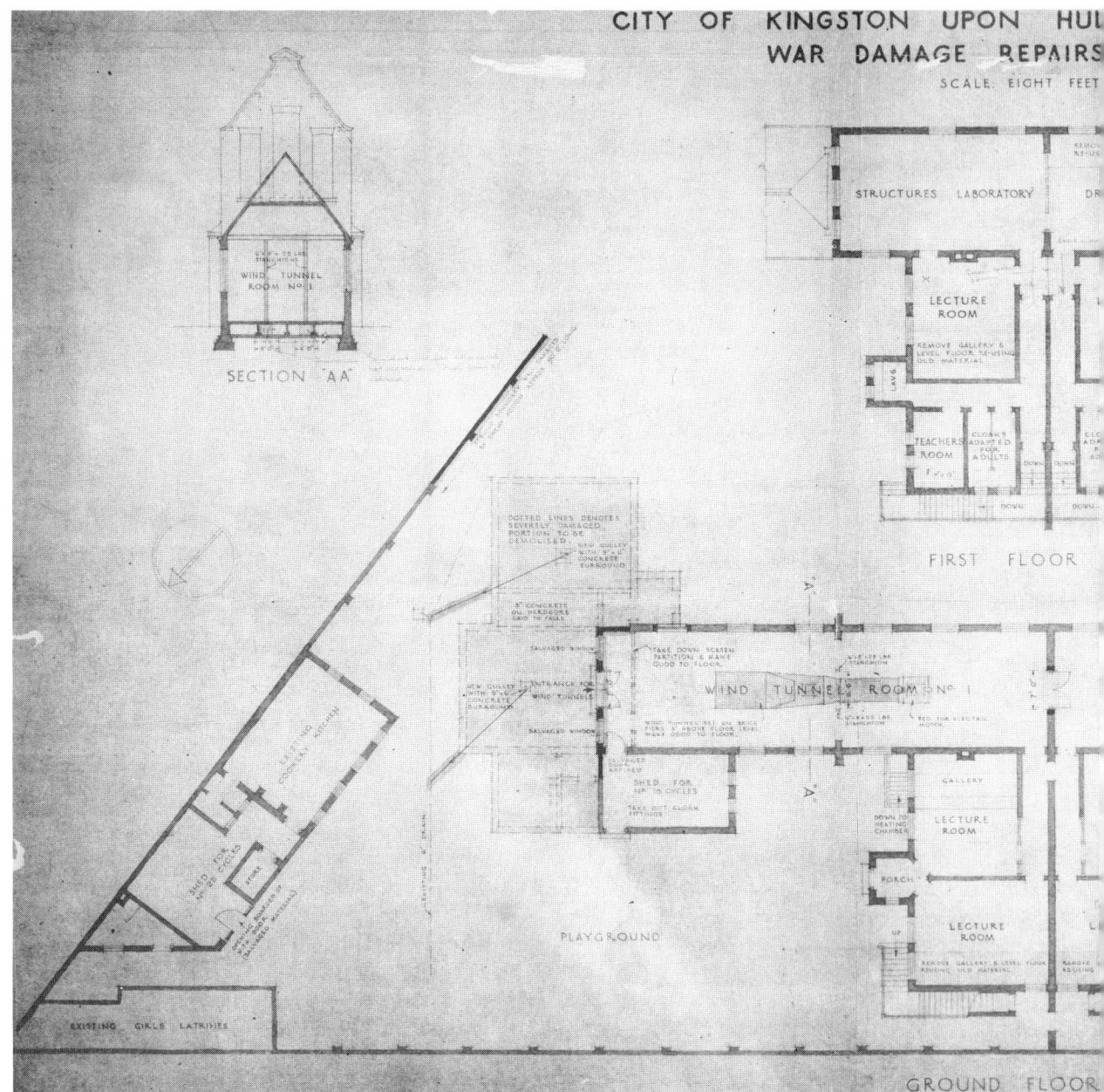

*Fig. 51.
Plan of
Middleton
Street
alterations,
1945*

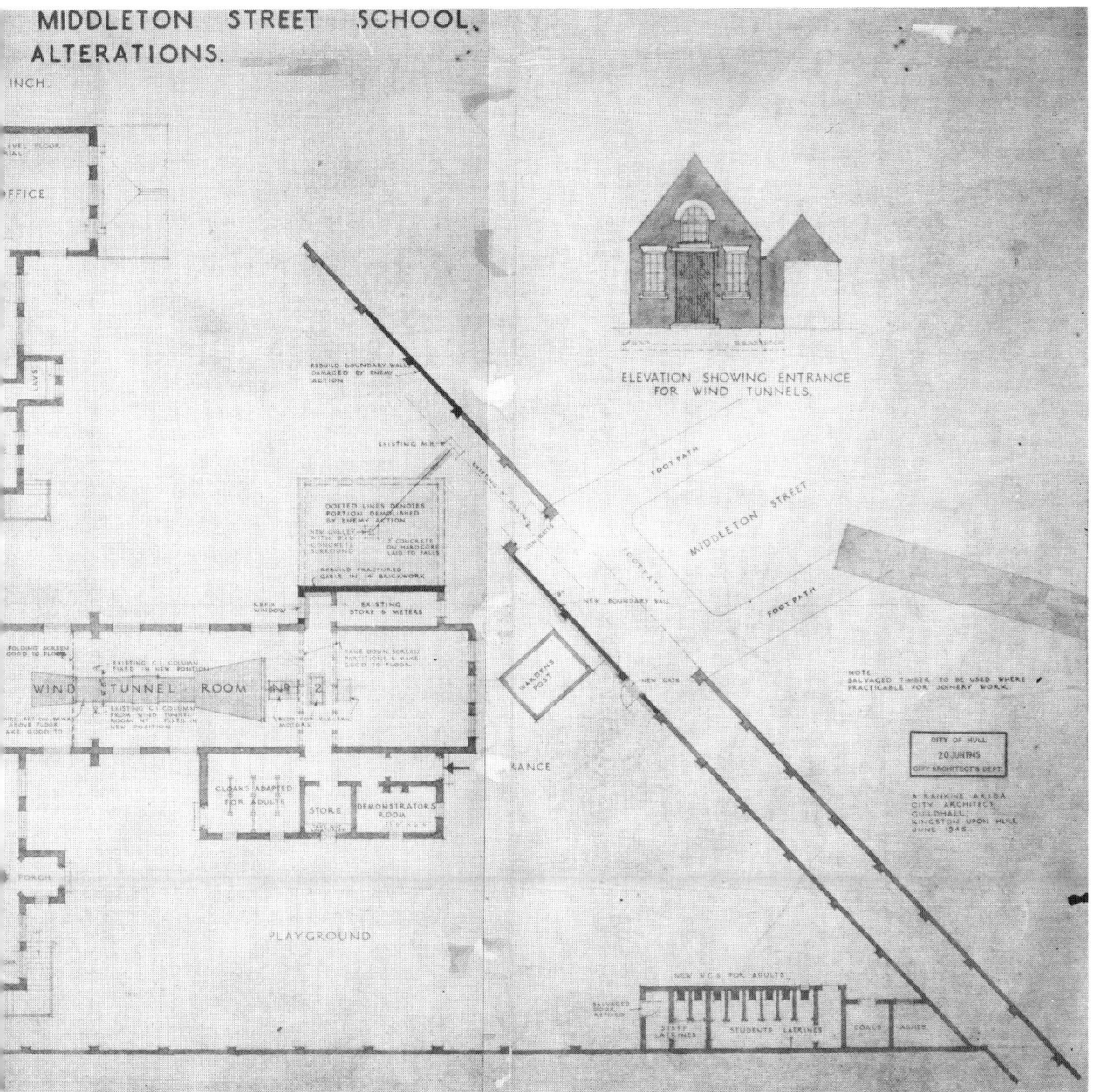

MIDDLETON STREET SCHOOL.
ALTERATIONS.

ELEVATION SHOWING ENTRANCE
FOR WIND TUNNELS.

£7325. From October 1945 the Diploma course in Aeronautics that had been a joint venture by the Technical College and the University College was transferred to the Technical College. From September 1945 new students on the course were charged 5 guineas per term for the first year and 6 guineas per term for the second year. The wind tunnel used by the University College was purchased for £463 and moved to Middleton Street in 1946. The revised estimated cost of adapting Middleton Street was now £2285 of which £1669 was for war damage repair and £616 for conversion.

In 1954 it was proposed to establish a sandwich course leading to the HND in Aeronautical Engineering. Students alternately spent six months at Technical College and six months in industry on the four year course. The HND was recognised by the Royal Aeronautical Society as exempting qualification from its Associate Fellowship Examination from 1961. When the workshop block at Queen's Gardens was completed in 1955 the Aeronautics course along with the two wind tunnels were transferred from Middleton Street. Staff were working on a supersonic wind tunnel at the time. In 1969 an experimental wind tunnel was built for the College by F. Singleton & Sons Ltd of Hull. The HND in Aeronautical Engineering had been merged into an HND Engineering course in September 1968

WORLD WAR TWO

From September 1939 classes for the Army in wireless work (field telegraphists and Morse operatives) were started. The Technical College was only allowed to take 250 evening students at a time due to the possibility of air raids and most schools were closed altogether for a short period. Courses for Army carpenters, fitters and turners started in 1940 and additional courses for · Engineering Cadets started in 1943. The staff could not cope with the extra demand and specialist outside teachers had to be recruited to some of the courses for servicemen.

The Senior Department was largely unaffected by the outbreak of war, however, the evening Classes were severely disrupted owing to the need to black out the College and provide adequate air raid protection. No classes started until the November with many not opening until the following January. Local industry responded well to the war and 44 firms released 137 students to attend the day classes in the engineering National Certificate during 1940.

During the war the number of building apprentices released for day classes almost trebled with 270 apprentices attending in 1944/45.

With the outbreak of the war the number of students attending evening classes inevitably fell but never went below 1400 students per week. The Trawler School had to close when its teacher, J. Taylor, left for munitions work; the Bakery School closed when G. Horton, the teacher, entered the army and the Wireless Courses were severely restricted as men between 17½ and 30 were not allowed to enrol. The applied natural science courses also closed for the duration of the war. Surprisingly all the evening courses were completed and final examinations held.

In 1941 the Ministry of Labour proposed a scheme to train disabled persons and pay £11 per class per week to the Technical College.

In 1942 a two year Junior Technical School course for the Building Industry was formed as part of Riley School for 60 boys and Osborne Street School repaired to take the classes. A Senior full time course in building was proposed for the 1943/44 session for the first time. The first 60 boys completed their Junior Building Trades Course in 1943/44 and little difficulty was found in placing them in the industry. Two RAF huts were bought for the Building Department at Osborne Street in 1945. In 1944/45 the two Junior Technical Schools were renamed the High School for Engineering and the High School for Building.

The peak year for evening class work occurred in 1937/38 when the number of students at the College reached 3400 with 293,765 student hours. At the end of the war the total number of students at the College had fallen to 3253.

POST WAR DEVELOPMENTS

Hairdressing courses run by the Technical College reopened in 1946 at Johnson - Broady, 23 Witham. It was proposed to move the classes to C. E. Barnes's premises at 23 Beverley Road in 1949. As the courses grew in popularity they were also provided with additional accommodation at Mrs Sugarman's, 104 Albert Avenue, from 1957. Mrs Sugarman was appointed Assistant Lecturer for Ladies Hairdressing in 1962. From October 1967 Mrs A Marshall's salon at 255 North

Boulevard was also hired for Monday morning practical work.

The new Ministry of Education suggested that the Technical College set-up a full time course for Sanitary Inspectors; the course started in July 1947 and charged a fee of £50 per student.

A course for the training of Merchant Navy personnel in Radar Maintenance was proposed in 1947. The Radar equipment was rented for £150 per annum and a course fee of 3 guineas was charged. A Radar Maintenance correspondence course was started in September 1952 at the request of the Ministry of Education with a fee of £10. New Radar equipment was rented from the Marconi Co. for £200 per annum in 1953.

Boot and shoe repairing evening classes were held in the footwear factory of H. Dalton in Charles Street in 1959.

The Worshipful Company of Turners awarded the Loveland Cup for Work in Wood jointly to the College and LCC Brixton School of Building in 1960. The following year a pupil from the Building Department won First Prize of the Silver Medal of the City and Guilds following the final examinations in Plumbing Work.

Mr A. Drake, a part time student from September 1958 to June 1962, was awarded the Silver Medal First Prize for being the best student in the City and Guilds first examination in Chemical Plant Operation for 1962. There was a Commonwealth Technical Training Week, organised by the City and Guilds, which commenced on the 29 April 1961 at the College.

Hull College of Technology (as the Technical College was known as from September 1955) became recognised as a Provincial Centre for the University of London External Degree Examinations in 1956. Fees were £2 10s per student for the whole or part exam and £1 5s for a single subject.

The College, along with four others, was invited by the Royal Institute of Chemistry to enter into a special relationship scheme under which the College would set its own paper for Part II of the Graduate Membership examination of the Institute in 1958 (a degree equivalent qualification). The College was recognised in the same year by the Institute of Physics for its study leading to membership of the Institute. Members of the Institute of Chemistry visited the College in July 1962 and were pleased with the well equipped chemical engineering laboratory and the panoramic view of Hull from the roof-top canteen. The Hull College of Technology applied to run courses for membership of the Institute of Biology Part II in 1971.

Some postgraduate work was offered in all departments of the College. In 1959 there was a visit to Sheffield University to discus possible projects for postgraduate research in the Mechanical Engineering department of the College. In 1961 equipment costing £500 was purchased for postgraduate work to be carried out at the College. A Lecturer in Physics, J. Moore, proposed to do some research work in collaboration with Hull University in 1963.

A research studentship was established in the Department of Chemistry and Biology in 1966/67 with a value of £500.

HIGH OR LOW LEVEL COURSES?

The Government White Paper of January 1961. 'Better opportunities in Technical Education', concentrated on lower level work in the colleges. Special courses for operatives were announced, craft courses were remodelled, the importance of technicians' courses was stressed

and new general courses were introduced.

As a response to the White Paper a department offering full and part time day release courses for school leavers was established at Park Street with Mr W. Lowe, former Principal of the Boulevard Evening Institute, as Head of Department. There was a full time pre-apprenticeship course in building for 20 boys aged 15 and a first year full time basic training course for engineering apprentices with 16 boys. In addition there were general engineering courses to give a common engineering grounding to all students with a total of 105 boys. The White Paper also led to an increase in the teaching staff at the College to meet the anticipated rise in student numbers. Twenty three new members of staff were appointed in July 1961 with many more later. The department at Park Street was abolished in 1968.

In November 1961 the student population taking advanced courses at the College was:

"Full time students
Higher National level
and above   66
Ordinary National level
& Advanced GCE   138
All full time students   452

Sandwich course students
Higher National level
and above   42

Part time students
Higher National level
and above   583
Ordinary National
& Advanced GCE   1508
All part time students   4613"[7]

These figures include over 60 students studying for degrees in engineering or general science. The sandwich courses were in chemical and aeronautical engineering. By 1963 there were around 650 full time and 6000 part time students taught by over 130 full time and 400 part time teachers. In 1967 this had risen to 206 full time staff, 60% of whom were graduates, and 350 part tine teachers teaching some 600 full time and 6000 part time students; most students came from a 30 mile radius of Hull although there were 40 overseas students.

During 1966 Hull College of Technology became the first in Yorkshire to install a computer. W. Stewart of Stafford was appointed Senior Lecturer in Mathematics for Computer Courses due to run from Easter 1966. The College initially hired an ICT Type 1202 Computer at an annual rent of £1800. The computer department continued to expand and later in 1966 the College bought time on the White Fish Authority's Elliot 903 computer for the City & Guilds 319 course, they also bought time on the Hull University computer from 1969.

The College became the second in Yorkshire to start a radiation physics course with its own laboratories. As early as 1956 the College of Technology had looked into the possibility of establishing a course in Atomic Energy and visited Harwell. Staff also went on a short course on measurement, handling and uses of radioactive isotopes. In 1964 the College was invited to participate in a Regional Advisory Scheme set-up by the Isotope Research Division of the Wantage Research Establishment to assist industry with problems on the use of isotopes. The following year it took part in a film, 'Eye for Isotopes', for the Atomic Energy Authority.

HULL COLLEGE OF FURTHER EDUCATION

In 1973-74 the College of Technology had nine departments of:

Building and Civil Engineering
Catering and allied studies
Chemistry and Biology
Electrical Engineering

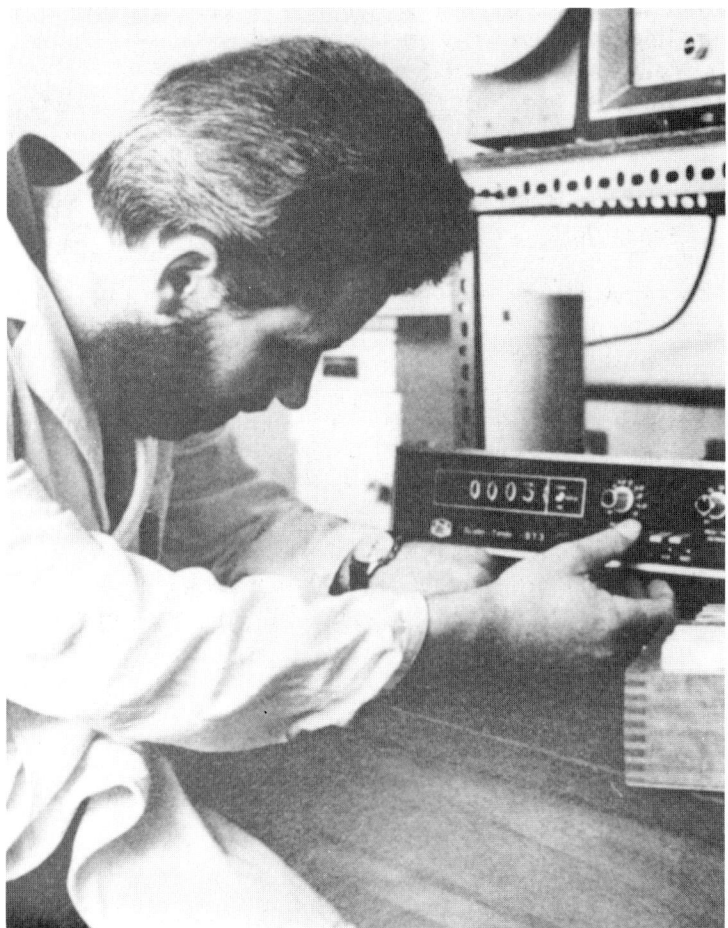

Fig. 52. Student conducting an experiment in the radioisotope laboratory (HC)

English and General Studies
Marine Engineering
Mathematics and Physics
Mechanical Engineering
Printing.

After reorganisation in 1976-77 the newly created Hull College of Further Education had seven departments:

Fig. 53. Business Studies Department (HC)

Secretarial Studies a new department with similar courses to the Business Studies Department of the former Commercial College).

The total number of students enrolling for courses at the College of Further Education in September 1976 was well above expectations and all departments worked to full capacity.

Full time	719
Sandwich	30
Block release	176
Part time Day	1360
Part time Day/Evening	2842
Evenings only	1746
Short Course	249
Link Course	111
Total	**7233**

Business Studies (formed mainly from Commercial Studies Department of the former College of Commerce).

Construction and Building Services (lost all ONC, OND and HND courses)

Engineering (divided into mechanical engineering, electrical engineering, fabrication & welding and the motor vehicle division).

Food and Fashion (formed from Catering and Allied Studies with some art classes from English & General Studies).

General Education and Liberal Studies (formed from English & General Studies Department of the C of T and the Social & Economic Studies Departments of the former College of Commerce).

Mathematics and Science (formed from the Chemistry & Biology and Maths. & Physics Departments of C of T with the Primary Residential Care Course from the College of Commerce and the Nursery Nursing Course from Bilton Grange High School).

Most Departments adapted quickly to the new organisation although the Department of Construction and Building Services had 300 fewer students due to the removal of its higher level courses. The Department also had problems caused by the reduction of the apprenticeship period for bricklayers, carpenters and joiners, which forced students to attend College in the evening as well as the day although were very reluctant to do so. A chronic lack of funds saw the department staff scouring demolition sites for reusable timber and bricks. The Engineering Department also commented that lack of staff and workshop space seriously limited the number of courses it was able to run.

From September 1977 the Department of Food and Fashion was upgraded from Grade III to Grade IV. The Department of Construction and Building Services was regraded from Grade IV to Grade V in 1979; regrading upwards reflected extra workload.

HCFE had also been given responsibility for educational provision at HM Prison, Hull, although no classes started in September 1976 due to riots at the prison. The Education Unit remained in staff hands during the riot but it was used as a rest room by the uniformed staff resulting in some losses of educational equipment. From 1980/81 the College also ran courses at HM Borstal Everthorpe.

The demand from students quickly outstripped the College of Further Education's ability to supply them with places. In 1977/78 Mr Tuck, the Principal, stated that, *"the College has been unable to respond to many of the demands made on it by industry, commerce, the schools, and government agencies such as the Manpower Services Commis-*

Fig. 54. The Building Department (HC)

sion, owing to its inability to provide additional accommodation."[8]

Extra demands were also made on the staff when new courses from the Technician and Business Education Councils had to be introduced for September 1978. These courses relied on different examination and assessment techniques from the older, exam orientated, courses placing much more emphasis on continual assessment. The courses attempted to combine numeracy and literacy by moving away from

single subject expertise to the student being able to use all their knowledge gained simultaneously on assignments. The Hull Colleges of Further and Higher Education were unable to agree on the provision of TEC courses although the College of Further Education was eventually recognised as the Centre for non-advanced TEC courses. The BEC and TEC were redesignated in 1983 as the Business and Technology Education Council (BTEC).

Two full time courses that had been run at Humberside College of Higher Education were transferred to the Secretarial Studies Department of HCFE in September 1980. The department now offered a range of full time secretarial courses from post-CSE to post-graduate level.

RE-ORGANISATION

Hull College of Further Education was restructured for September 1984 with three Faculties of, Technology; Business, Food and Caring Services and General and Alternative Education. The number of Departments under these new Faculties were increased from seven to nine:

- Business Studies
- General Education and Liberal Arts
- Engineering
- General Education, Mathematics and Science
- Secretarial Studies
- Alternative Education and Foundation Studies
- Building and Civil Engineering
- Catering and Caring Services
- Building, Electrical and Mechanical Services.

From the start of the summer term 1985 Hairdressing and Art and Design had become separate Divisions within the Faculty of Business, Food and Caring Services. Computing also became a separate Division from September 1985 within the Faculty of General and Alternative Education.

The largest reorganisation of HCFE since 1976 took place in 1987 with the general aim of the College being: *"To establish a further education system which enables the college to be responsive to the academic and vocational needs of individuals, industry, commerce and the community and, also, to respond quickly to changing needs and attitudes."*[9] The faculty system, established only three years previously, was replaced by ten departments with more emphasis placed on training; the Youth Training Services Department became the first college in Humberside to achieve full 'Approved Training Organisation' status in 1987. Adult and Youth Training Services merged in 1988 to form a new department.

In September 1988 the Engineering sector was merged with Science and the new Engineering and Science department also included a BTEC National Diploma course in Marine Telecommunications, transferred in September 1988 from Humberside College of Higher Education. The Marine Communications and Electronics courses were housed in part of the former Nautical College in George Street. Additionally, modules of courses in Engineering Applications and Processes were provided for students attending degree and HND courses locally.

In the Engineering sector the decline in the need for traditional engineering courses, particularly in the area of mechanical engineering and the increased need for expertise in electronics created an imbalance in the range of staff expertise available. This situation was resolved by premature retirements and some redeployment of staff.

Some further reorganisation took place in 1993 including the reintroduction of a Faculty system with each Faculty divided into three or more Schools. There are seven Faculties of Building & Civil Engineering, Engineering & Industrial Science (later shortened to Engineering), Business & Management Studies (later renamed Professional & Business Development), Continuing Education & Training, Design & Creative Studies, Health & Community Care and Hospitality, Leisure & Tourism. From 1993 the College started to run some higher education courses again, in modular form (it was hoped that all college courses would transfer to the modular system from 1993), including a BSc franchised from Hull University and HND's franchised from Humberside University.

Colleges could introduce new national schemes from 1993. National Vocational Qualifications are awarded to people in recognition, not of theoretical learning alone, but in their competence and skills at work. Linked with these work based schemes the new General Vocational Qualifications are part of a national scheme which allows students to build up a body of 'core' skills supported by additional options related to particular career and vocational specialisms. These GNVQ's are recognised by employers and by universities for entry to degree courses. Hull College can now offer a full range of courses at various levels and has, in some respects, regained its status as a 'straight through' institution incorporating many of the ideals of the original Hull Municipal Technical School.

Notes for Chapter Four

1.   Minutes of Hull Education Committee, 7 February 1905.

2.   Ibid.

3.   Ibid., 14 march 1905.

4.   Ibid., 9 July 1918.

5.   Ibid., Principal's Report to the H.E.C. 1927-28.

6.   Hull Daily Mail, 1938.

7.   R.H. Mitchell, The Development of Hull College of Technology from 1943 to 1973, University of Hull, 1975.

8.   Principal's Annual Report, Hull College of Further Education, 1978.

9.   Minutes of The Academic Board, H.C.F.E., 27 January 1987.

EVENING AND BRANCH SCHOOLS

Evening schools originally catered for students who had not passed through the elementary school and who needed basic instruction following the elementary school Code. By the 1890s these classes were becoming redundant, as compulsory schooling had been introduced in 1891, and it was recommended that the schools should be reorganised as evening continuation schools. Syllabuses became wider with classes in languages, science, art, handicrafts and domestic work. By 1898 these classes had become very popular and a separate Code for evening continuation schools became necessary. Technical, physical training and commercial courses were added and the upper age limit abolished. Grants also became available for attendance rather than examination results. In 1901 the administration of these schools was transferred to the Science and Art Department of the Board of Education. Local Education Authorities (i.e. Hull Corporation) took over control of evening continuation schools that had been organised by the School Board, Technical School or private bodies in 1902. The atten-

Fig. 55. Young Persons Literary and Christian Institute, Charlotte Street (HCM)

dance at the evening schools had been declining and the Hull Education Committee decided to bring them into 'organic connection' with the classes at the Technical and Art Schools for which they were considered as preparatory. After 1926 the evening continuation schools became Evening Institutes (which had existed since 1909) classified into Junior and Senior Institutes; Junior Institutes admitted pupils between fourteen and sixteen and the Senior Institutes took adult students.

An Act in 1899 had created the Board of Education, controlled by a President and Parliamentary Secretary; it replaced the Education Department, Charity Commission and the Department of Science and Art that had been competing national agencies.

The status of the Hull Technical Instruction Committee changed in 1898 when the Government authorised it to supervise the general work of science and art teaching and secondary education in

Hull. Gradually the Committee took over classes that had been provided by other organisations. The advanced courses at the Young People's Institute came under the control of the Committee from mid 1901. Most of their classes continued but the teachers were re-employed under better conditions, some classes were dropped as similar ones were already taught at the Technical School. The YPI became a Branch School for evening classes, the first of many annexes from Park Street. The following year saw a reduction in exam successes at the YPI and the Board of Education reduced its grant for Advanced Instruction in Science from 9½d to 9d.

Quite often students studying say mechanical engineering needed to have prior knowledge of mathematics, physics and machine drawing. To overcome this difficulty Manchester Technical School developed the group system in 1890; this allowed students to take a balanced combination of subjects and became adopted by other schools including Hull.

REORGANISATION OF THE EVENING SCHOOLS

In 1909 Luxton very perceptively stated that: "*In view of the ever increasing specialisation in most skilled trades and the greater competition among manufacturers, the general training of apprentices is becoming less every year, and the time appears to be rapidly approaching when the Technical School will be called upon to make up to some extent for the comparative failure of the apprenticeship system; this change to an evening trade school will certainly involve sacrifice on the part of the masters in the interests of their young employees and additional workshop equipment within the School itself.*"[1]

In 1909 the Board of Education ordered the evening schools to be reorganised. At three convenient centres there would be established Branch Technical and Commercial Schools, providing first year technical and second year commercial courses. Much of the elementary work done at the main Technical School at Park Street would be transferred to them and domestic science schools would be set-up with girls under 17 excluded from the corresponding classes at the main Technical School. One branch school would be the YPI - all their higher work to be removed to the main Technical School so the distinction between the two institutions would become much clearer.

The new Institutes were seen as preparing students for the Technical School. To encourage elementary school leavers 100 scholarships were to be offered.

Luxton supervised the establishment of the evening institutes although some decentralisation had already occurred with the branch commercial school at the YPI. Commercial branch schools were set-up at Boulevard Secondary School, Craven Street and the YPI with technical branch schools in the same buildings. The structure of the courses was very progressive and introduced the grouped course system. For the first three years of a four or five year course students could choose a range of appropriate subjects and then specialise in the final years. The courses were made compulsory for three evenings a week to increase the number of successful students.

Some courses at the Technical School had experimented with grouped classes over the past seven years but without any compulsory element. This system had been unrecognised by the Board of Education but Luxton hoped that they would see its benefits and from 1910 they did. Compulsory courses did lead to a fall in the number of students as the hours of work the employers demanded, 6 am to 6 pm

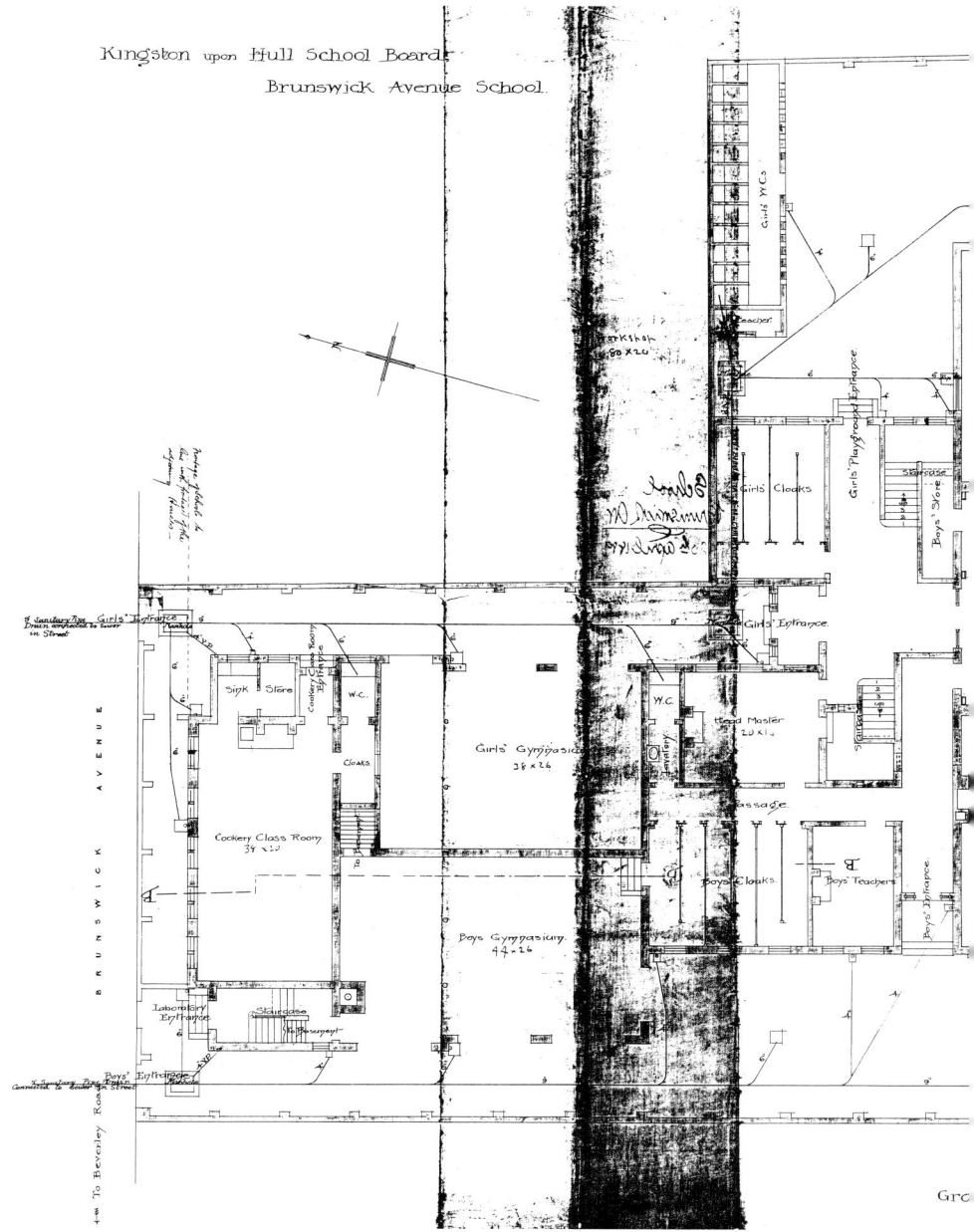

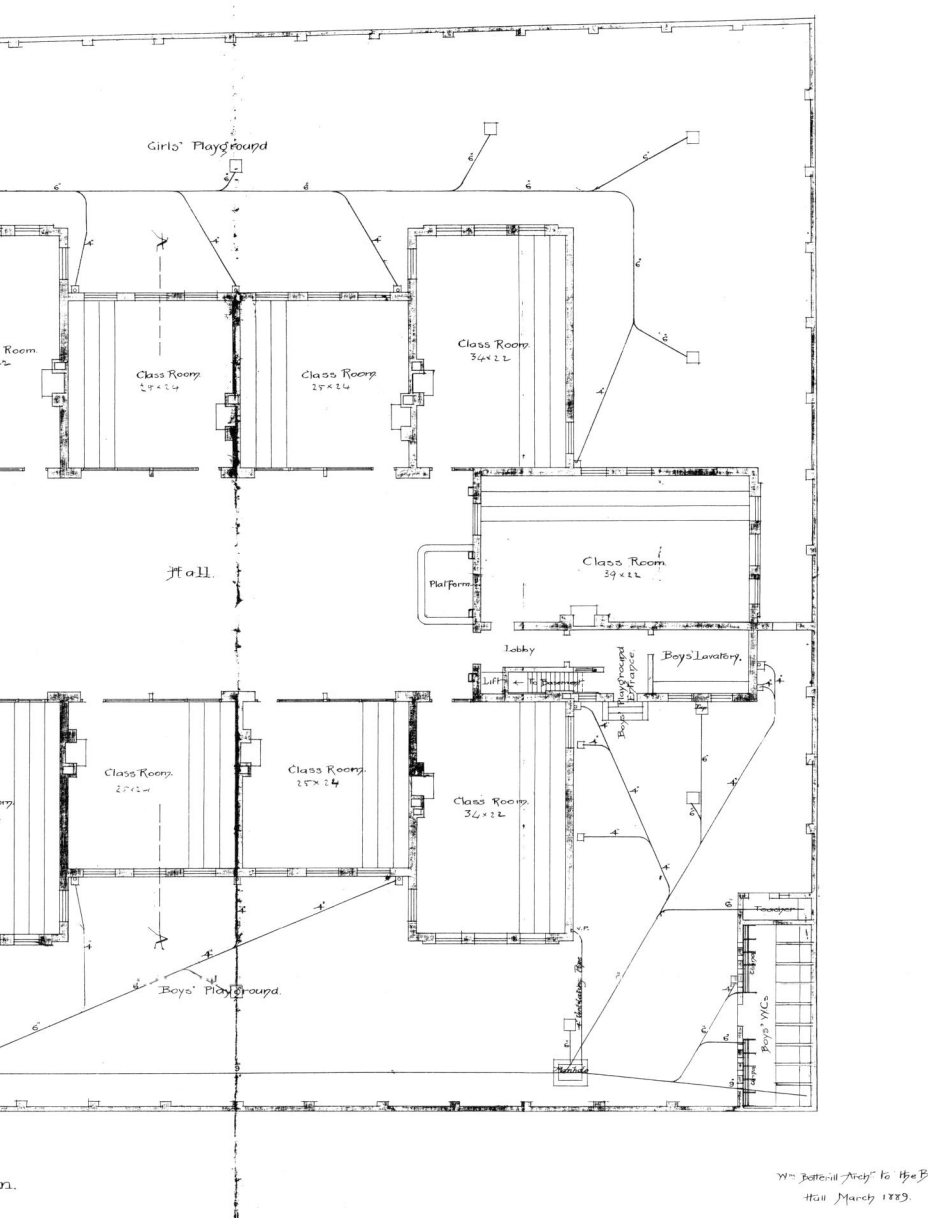

Girls' Playground

Room.

Class Room.
29×24

Class Room.
25×24

Class Room.
34×22

Hall.

Class Room
39×22

Platform

Lobby

Lift

Boys' Lavatory.

Class Room.
29×24

Class Room.
25×24

Class Room.
34×22

Boys' Playground.

Boys' W.Cs

Wᵐ Betterill Archᵗ to the Board
Hull March 1889.

*Fig. 56.
Brunswick
Avenue
Central
Board
School, this
later became
the home of
the
Commercial
School
(KHRO)*

or 8 am to 8 pm, made evening classes seem very unattractive. Some potential students went to private schools or took correspondence courses but the instruction they received was well below that of the Technical School. For the first year, 1910, there were 246 entries at the technical branch schools with 158 of them passing in three out of four subjects and qualifying for entry to the Technical School; for the commercial schools there were 556 entries with 253 passes.

For the branch commercial schools to be successful they needed a School of Commerce to transfer to for the final years of their courses. In September 1911 the Central School of Commerce opened in Brunswick Avenue, administered as part of the Technical College, when the High School for Girls moved out. All evening commercial classes were transferred from Park Street and in its first year the numbers rose from 947 to 1029. Newland Avenue School became an additional branch commercial school from 1911 with Middleton Street and Villa Place Schools added the following year to relieve pressure on the YPI. Sidmouth Street also became a branch commercial school from 1914/15.

The isolated Domestic Evening Schools were discontinued in 1914 and reorganised in a more centralised form and on a more technical basis at Boulevard, Craven Street and Central Secondary Schools. The Day Technical Institute at Park St. was still not progressing mainly because there was little industrial employment for men over 18. The 12 hours work demanded by many local employers remained a serious handicap and Luxton commented that *"the wonder is that many boys should be courageous enough to attend Evening Classes"*.[2] The Bookkeeping teachers had objected to the grouped course system and only partially implemented it; their poor exam results compared to the rest of the commercial classes reflected that.

Branch Domestic Science Schools taught English, dressmaking, millinery, cookery, music and singing, physical exercises, needlework, embroidery and at one school ambulance work. There were five such schools, by 1916, at Craven Street, Boulevard, Central, Sidmouth Street and Constable Street with attendances of 838 for 1914/15 and 1683 for 1915/16.

In the evening schools numbers had increased from 2377 in 1909/10 to 3051 in 1913/14 and the grant from the Board of Education had been increased by 61%.

CHANGES AT THE AFFILIATED SCHOOLS

In 1919 Luxton proposed that Summer Courses should be run in some commercial subjects in the Evening Schools. There would be no fee but students would have had to attend a proper course in the winter. He also proposed that Teachers' Training Courses should be run in the summer at the Technical School. Fees were charged from 1922 for the summer classes.

The School of Commerce was reorganised for the 1920/21 session with an upper and a lower school. The lower school taught the usual subjects while the upper school had more specialised courses linked to the important trades in Hull and classes for the Bankers' Institute, the Insurance Institute, the Faculty of Insurance and various university examinations. The lower school was open on Monday, Wednesday and Friday evenings and the upper school opened on Tuesday and Friday evenings. The YPI was also slightly reorganised with the appointment of H. Williams as the single headmaster for both the Technical and Commercial Schools. Compulsory physical education had been introduced in the Branch Schools the previous year but the attendance was very poor so it was decided to revert to a voluntary system.

The education offices in Albion Street were soon to be given up and in 1924 the Hull Education Committee still thought that the proposals for day continuation schools outlined in the 1918 Education Act might come into force. Luxton suggested that the offices should be used for a Central School of Commerce for Girls. However, the Corporation did not think that they could be used for education purposes and proposed to sell or let the building.

An attempt to run an advanced commercial course in 1923/24 met with failure as employers would not give students any preference. There was no point attending a course when employment was more attractive.

The number of students attending the Branch Technical Schools gave cause for concern in 1921. Only 260 pupils attended the four schools and Luxton recommended a single headmaster to replace the four separate headmasters. Supplies of students from the Branch Commercial Schools to the lower school of the School of Commerce were also unsatisfactory. The Free Admission Card Scheme had not produced any increase from the previous year;

children failed to utilise their cards until they secured employment with the result that the cards had lapsed and they had to pay fees.

In the Branch Commercial Schools Luxton felt that the teachers were not experimenting with new teaching techniques but still putting all the emphasis on passing the final exam. This lack of flexibility would lead to poorer examination results.

The evening class admissions for 1925 were abnormally large and an additional Domestic Science School opened at Somerset Street and a commercial course opened at Beverley Road to relieve pressure on Middleton Street.

Non-vocational Institutes were established in 1928/29 after Bates had visited the London Institutes, the first opened at Williamson Street for men to study craft, literary, social and economic topics with the intention that it should become self governing in time. By 1928 there were over 10,000 students in the evening classes and an additional Women's Institute had to be opened at Thoresby Street School followed by one at Escourt Street (formerly Craven Street) for the new East Hull housing estate. The East Hull Men's Institute (Williamson Street) had over 200 members in 1929 and two new Institutes at

Sidmouth Street (Newland Literary Institute) and Lincoln Street (Wilmington Junior Men's Institute) were opened. A new Men's Evening Institute opened at Francis Askew School in 1930/31 as did the nucleus of a Women's Institute. Additional Women's Institutes opened at Flinton Grove, Hall Road and Mersey Street Schools and a new Men's Institute opened at Hall Road in 1931/32. A new Young Men's Institute opened as a section of the Craven Street Evening School for the 1934/35 session with the fee set at 6d for the winter classes.

The Boulevard Evening School had expanded during 1928 with an orchestra, school magazine, 'The Boulevesco', and it had introduced a house system to encourage team work and loyalty to the School.

Bates commented on the Evening Institutes in 1929. *"The activities of the institutes are too various to be described in a few words, but their cultural effect on adolescent life has an enormous and growing influence on the development of mind and manners among the younger generation, to whom these institutes are more and more becoming the 'People's College' or the 'Home from home'."*[3]

The Evening Institutes continued to expand rising from 8 in 1925 to 20 in 1931 and student numbers increased from 5598 to almost 10,000 over the same period. There was a decrease in numbers at the Evening Institutes during 1932/33 due to a decrease in apprenticeships, short time work and the consequent lack of money to spent on further education.

The Co-operative Society decided to discontinue their general education classes in Hull (which were probably held in Osborne Street School) and send their employees to the Commercial Evening Institutes. There were enough students to start a new institute and Osborne Street School was opened for the Co-op's senior students as a Branch Commercial Evening Institute for the Distributive Trades in October 1930.

The Central School of Commerce had become so full by 1928/29 that most of the lower grade classed had to be moved to the Grammar School where they attracted some ex-Grammarians. The Grammar School was opened as an additional Branch Commercial School in 1929/30. Special commercial classes were opened in 1930/31 for unemployed clerical students. The course was quite successful and placed nearly 30 boys and girls in employment after the first year.

Following a survey of technical and commercial education in Hull in 1928, by the Board of Education, there were some staff changes. Bates would no longer be in charge of supervising evening schools (Bates had been appointed Assistant Organiser in July 1925) except those at the Technical College; Mr Machin was to be relieved of all duties as headmaster of the Central School of Commerce (he had been headmaster since 1927 when he replaced E. P. Bates) and assistant master at Riley High but take over organisation of all evening institutes, under the general supervision of Mr Bates for two years, and become an inspector of elementary schools; the School of Commerce would have a new Principal in charge of day and evening work with the exception of the Domestic Science and Manual Instruction Centres. Mr Machin took up his new posts from 10 June 1930 and Allan F. George was appointed Principal of the College of Commerce from July 1930. The College

Fig. 57. Osborne Street Board School during the Second World War.
(KHRO)

Fig. 58. The College of Commerce, Queen's Gardens. (RB)

side University, and by 1989 the Queen's Gardens site had been taken over by Hull College of Further Education. It is now the Wilberforce Block of Hull College.

Notes for Chapter Five

1.   Minutes of Hull Education Committee, 12 October 1909.

2.   Ibid., 9 June 1914.

3.   Ibid., Principal's Report to H.E.C., 1928-29.

of Commerce had been administered with the Evening Institutes but was now a separate institution and recognised as a College for Further Education by the Board of Education. Colleges for Further Education were the colleges controlled by local authorities for vocational further education.

In March 1931 the Hull Education Committee thought the former Poor Law Offices in Anlaby Road/Harley Street could be used for day and evening courses in commerce. However, by July they had decided that the premises were unsuitable. By April 1932 discussions were being held with the Board of Education on the reorganisation of Brunswick Avenue to provide day courses in commerce. The Brunswick Avenue Central School gradually closed whilst the College of Commerce expanding its day work

The College of Commerce moved to newly constructed premises in Queen's Gardens in the early 1970s. In 1976 the College became part of Humberside College of Higher Education, now Humber-

JUNIOR TECHNICAL SCHOOLS

Junior technical schools essentially covered the gap between the school leaving age of 13/14 and apprenticeships. The Schools became recognised as a separate form of instruction by the Board of Education in 1913; at the time there were 194 Junior Schools in the country including 44 junior commercial and 15 junior housewifery schools and usually they had less than 200 pupils. They were "*definitely not intended to provide courses furnishing a preparation for the professions, universities or higher further technical training, they are intended to prepare pupils for artisan or other employment*".[1] The courses were full time taking pupils who have decided to enter a particular type of industrial work but not a specific occupation within an industry.

The curriculum provided a preparation for industrial and commercial employment with continued general education. Teachers usually had some workshop experience and lectured in the evening institutes.

Because fees were payable in grammar schools, and were higher than those in junior technical schools, parents tended to assume that a grammar school education was something intrinsically superior, fees in junior technical schools were fixed at £5 in 1926.

It was not until 1 April 1945, as a result of the 1944 Education Act, that junior technical, commercial and art schools were recognised as secondary technical schools and absorbed into the state education system. At the time there were around 300 Junior Schools with about 65,000 pupils. Recognition led to more able students attending the schools at 11 instead of 13, eliminating the 'creaming off' selection methods of the 11 plus.

A UNIQUE SCHOOL

In his 1894 report on the Hull Technical Instruction Committee's Scheme for providing Technical Instruction Dr Riley, the Technical School's Director of Studies and Organising Secretary, envisaged a 2 year full time Junior Technical School (to be a department of the Technical School) "*for the preparatory training of those of lower attainments*".[2]

For the first year that figures are available, 1894, there were 27 junior technicals and 12 junior commercials at the Junior School. The School moved, along with the rest of the Technical School, to Park Street in 1898.

From 1900 the Junior Department of the Technical School would only take pupils for more than three terms. Previously parents had been placing boys in the school for short periods until they gained employment, which had led to a great deal of disorganisation.

The Junior School expanded rapidly and in 1903 admitted 74 boys taking either a three year course in commerce and modern languages (41) or a two year course in general engineering (33). Both courses gradually became extended to five years and the entry age lowered to eleven plus although little emphasis was placed on examination results.

After the Hull Education Committee became the Local Education Authority in 1903 the Junior

School operated as an 'A' School on the recommendations of the Board of Education. The School differed from normal 'A' Schools in that the 3rd and 4th years were taken at the Technical Institute instead of courses usually taught at the Junior School; this unique arrangement was to cause problems for the School until 1945.

The Head Master of Hymers College, Mr Gore, was strongly opposed to the continued existence of the Junior School and in 1904 Riley had to justify the School financially and educationally. The two senior technical departments of the Technical School required a staff of nine costing £1760 per year. Expenditure on apparatus and materials was around £2000 per annum. There were 37 day students taking full technical courses - fees amounted to £580 and grant from the Board of Education was £290 - leaving a debit balance of £1130 per year. By employing three extra staff at £420 per year it was feasible to conduct a secondary day school (the Junior Department) of 120 boys producing £378 in fees and £680 in grants - thus reducing the debit to £492. The Technical School could also employ these three teachers to conduct evening classes producing a revenue of £200 in fees and grants. There was a slight expenditure of around £60 on materials, prizes, etc. leaving a final debit balance of only £352 per year.

For 1904 the Government Inspectors reports were quite favourable to the Hull Junior School *"good systematic work is being done in science, mathematics and the teaching reaches a high standard. The organisation of the school is excellent."*[3]

The curriculum taught at the Junior School was not strictly technical in that it did not teach the application of pure science to industrial processes. The course included English, maths and the elementary principles of chemistry, physics and mechanics with drawing and manual instruction.

In teaching drawing real parts of machinery were copied instead of the more conventional designs such as Acanthus leaves. Nearly all the students of the senior technical courses who distinguished themselves had received their preliminary training in the Junior School.

Immediate Origin of Boys in the Technical Departments 1904

Junior School	13
Local Higher Grade Schools (including Grimsby)	3
Hymers College	3
Hull Grammar School	1
Outside Secondary Schools	17

The Principal of the Technical School, Mr Luxton, was proud of the Junior School and thought that it was appreciated by employers because the boys were active physically and mentally, adaptable and free from the *"swelled head"*[4] of normal youth. He thought the School could be described as a secondary school as it provided most of the elements of a secondary education apart from art and gymnastics. The organisation of the School was unique and was used as a model for some other schools nationally *"with a bias towards commerce or the constructive trades"*[5] after 1909.

A scheme for awarding internal College Diplomas and Certificates had started in 1910 and fully developed by 1912. There was a Diploma exam for students of at least two years standing in the Senior Day Departments and a School Leaving Certificate for

Municipal Technical College,

— Park Street, Hull. —

———

Founded 1894.

———

Riley High School

(Technical and Commercial).

———

Headmaster—

W. S. COOPER, B.Sc., Hons. (London), A.I.C.

———

*Enquiries relative to the entry of boys into the Day School should
be addressed to the Headmaster.*

Tel. 33648.

1,000-6-20—H.P.L.—c1930.

Fig. 59. *Fronticepiece from Riley High School Prospectus, 1930.*
(HC)

boys of at least three years standing in the Junior Day Departments.

The Junior Department of the Hull Technical College became recognised as a separate form of instruction by the Board of Education in 1913. Hull's school was quite unique in that courses were for four years rather than the normal two or three and it was hoped that pupils would progress to the Technical College courses. The Board would only recognise three year courses and gave the Hull Technical College until 1916 to reorganise. The College responded and extended the senior courses by starting a new general one year course to act as a buffer between the Junior Day School and the Day Technical Institute. The new first year course attracted 37 students when ran for the first time in 1916.

A rigid age limit of 12½ - 13½ for entry to the Junior Day School was imposed by the Board of Education for the 1916/17 session for the first time. Luxton thought this had a disastrous effect on the boys and the College; large numbers of able students had to be turned away effectively ending their day school education at 14. The 'organic link' between the Junior School and the Senior Department had been broken, removing the only adequate supply of well-trained boys for the senior school.

SOCIAL DEVELOPMENTS

During the 1913/14 session the Junior School went on its first annual excursion, to Lincoln, and Mr Bates founded the Junior Library. The Junior Library contained 800 volumes by 1925 although it was only open at 12 noon on Mondays and Wednesdays and each afternoon at 4.30.

Physical education also became part of the curriculum for the first time in the Junior School in 1913.

Social activities at the Junior School continued to prosper with a choir, photographic society, games and athletics plus an annual sports day held in mid May or June. The Junior choir and orchestra attracted 108 men and 92 women in 1925.

There was also a *"great adventure"*[6] to London in 1923. Tom Jeffrey, a pupil at the time, remembers Mr Luxton standing in front of the whole school and saying: "There are still rogues of both sexes in London. On no account leave your group nor speak to anyone." A party of staff and students went on a trip to Paris during the May 1925 holiday.

A NEW SCHOOL?

Plans were drawn up for a new Junior Technical School on the Cottingham site (where it had been hoped to develop the Senior Technical College/ University College) in April 1924; but before permission could be granted the Board of Education requested a meeting with Hull Education Committee representatives. The Board suggested that the new school should be recognised as a secondary not a junior school, although the character of the school would not be altered, and take pupils from 11 plus to 16, instead of

Fig. 60. Riley Pupils (HC)

13 to 15 or 16. They also suggested that the school should have a separate headmaster and be limited to 500 pupils; the Hull representatives objected to the latter two proposals but without effect. The new school should have been complemented by a similar one in East Hull (Craven Street Secondary School when transferred to new premises). The Board also gave the impression that the existing Junior School could be recognised as a secondary school even if it did not move, this pleasantly surprised the Hull Education Committee. However, after discussions the Board decided that the Junior School should continue as before until the retirement of the Principal.

The Hull Education Committee decided to appoint an Assistant Organiser of Evening Classes in 1925 who would take over the Park Street Evening Technical College when the Principal of the Technical College, Mr Luxton, retired. An independent Principal could then be appointed to the proposed new Secondary School. E. P. Bates was appointed Assistant Organiser in July 1925. However, the Board replying to the request to change recognition

of the Junior Department from a junior to a secondary school, in August 1926, refused permission as they thought Park Street premises to be unsuitable for a secondary school and that the Junior School would continue to be recognised as before, although they appreciated the unique nature of the school.

Luxton resigned in December 1925 to take effect from the end of the school year (31 July 1926). The retirement obviously required some reorganisation; W. S. Cooper, second master of the Junior Day School, was appointed Head Master in independent control (from the Principal of the Technical School) of the school. The new Day 'Secondary' School was renamed Riley High School in November 1926. The Board of Education suggested it should just be named Riley School but the Committee ignored them. The school still formed part of the Technical College according to the Board.

In December 1929 the Committee again revived the idea of building a new Riley High School on the Technical College playing fields on Cottingham Road. The decision to proceed with the plans was, not

surprisingly, continually deferred. The Committee again applied to the Board of Education for recognition of Riley High School as a secondary school from 1 September 1931. The Board replied that they would only recognise the school if it moved to separate premises. In May 1940 the Committee proposed to erect the new Riley School on the new Bilton Grange Estate, however, the Board of Education refused permission until at least the end of the war.

Some streaming of the pupils of Riley High School had been introduced in 1925/26 much to the benefit of the slow learners. At the time 250 boys took engineering courses and 350 took commercial courses.

As a result of the reorganisation in 1926 Riley High could not be recognised by London University for General School Examinations but the Northern Universities Joint Matriculation Board agreed that the School could take their examinations from 1928. After a general inspection by HM Inspectors in 1930 the school developed more and more on the lines of the secondary school and a sixth form aiming at the Higher School Cer-

Fig. 61. Riley pupils visiting the Triangle Garage on Anlaby Road
(HC)

In 1936 a number of pupils were transferred to the College of Commerce and shorthand, bookkeeping and typewriting disappeared from the curriculum so that by 1939 the school was almost indistinguishable in scope from a grammar school with modern and science sides.

THE SECOND WORLD WAR

Most Hull schools closed at the beginning of the war but gradually reopened when they had adequate air raid shelters; Malet Lambert and Newland High Schools reopened in December 1939 and the premises were used to give half-time instruction to Riley, Kingston and the Grammar school pupils. Riley attended Malet Lambert in the mornings only. Riley School in Park Street and its South Myton annexe (Adelaide Street) were reopened in early 1940 after they had been provided with air raid protection. A large number of Riley pupils had to be evacuated to Bridlington in the September following the outbreak of war followed by a second move to Drax and a third to the Percy Jackson Grammar School in Doncaster all in the same year; this

tificate Examination was established.

Riley High School introduced the house system in 1928/29 to promote closer contact between staff and scholars; the four houses were Humber, Newton, Faraday and Kingston. Points were awarded for work and sport and in the first year Newton House won the 'House Shield' with 5616 points.

After 1933 pupils were charged fees of £6 6s per annum or £2 2s per term, this amount included 10s 6d for games and social activities. Part of the Artillery Barracks in Park Street was used by Riley pupils for additional physical training from 1938.

In the early 1930s a new department was added to the school, the 2-year engineering course with entry at the age of 13 years, subsequently known as the High School for Engineering. This added to the numbers and to the difficulties of finding accommodation.

obviously led to serious difficulties organising the school work.

In 1942 a Junior Technical School for the Building Industry was formed as part of Riley School and Osborne Street School repaired to take the classes. The first 60 boys completed their Junior Building Trades Course in 1943/44 and little difficulty was found in placing them in the industry. Two RAF huts were bought for the Building Department at Osborne Street in 1945.

SECONDARY SCHOOL STATUS

The 1944 Education Act required the Council to produce a development plan for education. On the technical side two junior technical schools for girls were planned and the existing junior technical schools were to be rehoused as technical high schools of engineering, building, commerce, art and crafts and nautical training. Riley High School was also to move to the former Boulevard School as a secondary high school. At the secondary high school level Newton Hall and Kelvin Hall were created as mixed technical high schools in combination with

modern schools on a campus. Kelvin Hall, opened in 1959, originally had accommodation for 600 pupils and with Wyke Hall mixed secondary modern school formed Bricknell High School. Newton Hall, opened in 1957, also accommodated 600 pupils and with Elizabeth Hall and Shakespeare Hall formed Greatfield High School. Trinity House Navigational School also became a technical high school.

Riley High School and the High School for Engineering separated from the Technical College in 1947 to form a new High School

Fig. 62. Riley High School, Boulevard (The Boulevardian)

housed in the former Kingston High School premises in the Boulevard. Edwin Harrison was appointed temporary Acting Head Master of Riley and the High School for Engineering from 1 April 1945. Herbert Rochester, of Kenilworth, became Head Master of the separately administered Riley High School from October 1947.

The School remained in the Boulevard until it transferred to new buildings erected in Parkfield Drive in 1957. The School was officially opened by Eric Turner, Chairman of Blackburn and General Aircraft Ltd on 1 November 1957 as Riley Technical High School. It had been designed by the City Architect and built by Robinson & Sawdon Ltd of Hull.

The 2-year Engineering course (i.e. the old High School for Engineering) was discontinued when Riley High moved but the new school provided for boys from the age of eleven onwards with a full secondary technical school course with an engineering bias. The aim of the school was "to give a good general education with some technical insight and to maintain

Fig. 63. Riley Technical High School, Parkfield Drive, 1957 (HC)

the high academic standards by means of a curriculum and approach that meets the demands of a new age."[7]

By 1988 the School had closed and ironically Hull College of Further Education took over the premises as the Riley Centre. It was refurbished in 1990/91 and today is home to Caring and Performance Arts besides other courses.

Notes for Chapter Six

1. Board of Education Report, 1912-13.
2. Minutes of the Technical Instruction Committee, 6 April 1894.
3. Minutes of Hull Education Committee, 7 February 1905.
4. Ibid., 12 October 1909.
5. Ibid., 16 November 1909.
6. Ibid., Principal's Report to the H.E.C. 1922-23.
7. Opening of Riley Technical High School, 1957.

EARLY CLASSES[1]

There had been no provision for technical classes for fishermen when the Hull Municipal Technical School started in 1893 as the Technical Instruction Committee thought that the Trinity House School provided the necessary navigation classes. Since 1889 Skippers and Second Hands of trawlers over 20 tons had had to pass a simple examination but some form of instruction was still needed. After consulting other technical institutes the Committee decided to ask the Hull Smack Owners Association and the Hull Trawl Fishermen's Protective Society for their suggestions on classes. The fishermen's representatives thought that navigation classes should be held and scientific lectures delivered on the habits and food of fishes; they also offered to let St Andrew's Hall in West Dock Street to hold the classes in pisciculture and navigation. The Technical Instruction Committee agreed and appointed Reuben Manton, from Grimsby, as teacher and the first, free, classes started in Spring 1895. At first the navigation classes, held in a room above St Andrew's Hall, were popular with an average attendance of 12, however by the Winter session the attendance had fallen to only 3. Most students were too tired after doing their normal work to attend evening classes. The following year 151 students enrolled in the Fishermen's Classes although the average attendance was only 6.7. It was stated that the purpose of the classes was to provide instruction in *"Navigation, Nautical Astronomy and Seamanship"[2]* but in effect the early curriculum was dominated by elementary arithmetic, chartwork and compass work.

Mr Manton actively promoted the classes and spent much of his spare time on the dock enticing men to join the classes, he also wrote the textbook used in the

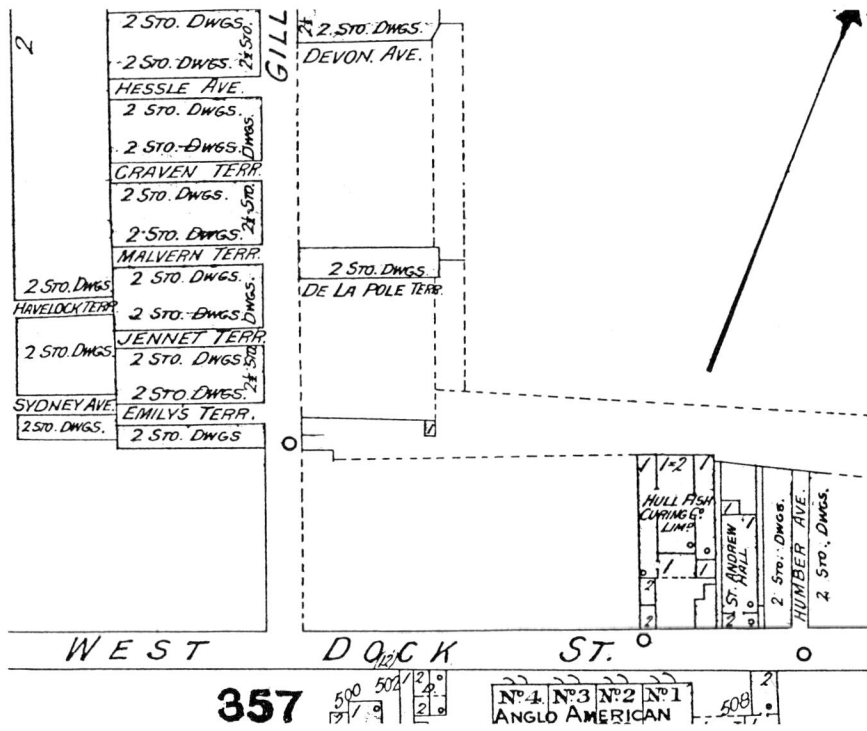

Fig. 64. *Goad's Insurance Plan showing St Andrew's Hall, West Dock St., 1893*

classes. Manton also thought that the classes should take place every day so more potential pupils could use it. As a result of his efforts discussions took place with the Hull Fishing Owner's Association who suggested a move to *"neutral territory"*[3] on Hessle Road. The Committee rented a house and shop on the east corner of Hessle Road and Harrow Street from January 1899, they sublet the shop to a china dealer who also ran the pawnbroker's on the opposite side of Harrow Street.

Classes started on 31 January in the new School for Fishermen and Manton received an increased salary of £2 per week. In those days the School for Fishermen provided two main services for fishermen - short courses for fishermen who were between trips and longer courses, held in the afternoon and evening, for those intending to join the fishing industry. The syllabus at first was very elementary. It was not even essential that the candidate should be able to read or write; he could be *"com-*

pletely ignorant of the three R's"[4] and yet pass the examination. New regulations that placed more emphasis on navigation came into force in 1906. Pupils had the opportunity to study for the Board of Trade's Certificates but instruction was not mainly to this end.

The School was normally open for forty-eight weeks in the year and the number of students using the facilities grew from about 400 in 1906 to well over 650 by 1912. Over the same period the number of students attending each day increased from about fourteen to forty - although the number of hours each student spent in the school during the year was only twenty-five or so. About 10% of trawlermen enrolled at the School by 1907 and classes still took place in only three small rooms.

The School for Fishermen gradually expanded and by January 1908 an assistant instructor for the evenings, Frederick Barnes, had to be appointed. Barnes had been working voluntarily at the School and was an ex-pupil, passing the Extra Skippers Certificate with Honours.

Fig. 65. Harrow Street, formerly the Fishermen's School. (KHRO)

Many men attended for years and still found the school useful as a place for advice or instruction after they had left. The Board of Education also thought highly of Manton. *"The Instructor is a man of exceptional qualification for the post which he occupies, and he possesses a rare enthusiasm in his work ... For many years he has worked uncomplainingly under great difficulties."*[5]

A NEW SCHOOL

The Board of Education commented very favourably on the School for 1906/07 and suggested that a new school might be necessary and that grants were available.

After consulting with the Hull Fishing Vessel Owners Association Ltd. in 1909 the Hull Education Committee decided to build a new trade school as quickly as possible. The new School would ideally consist of two stories the lower story would contain a net room, store room, stow room, cloakroom and lavatory. The upper story would contain classrooms for certificated men, senior weekly hands, junior weekly hands and learners with an instructor's room and cloakroom. The roof had to be flat to take a wheelhouse, mast and rigging.

Fig. 66. The former Nautical School, Boulevard. (RB)

Several sites for the new School were looked at in Daltry Street, Hessle Road and South Parade but they all proved to be unsuitable. In 1909 the Committee put in an offer for 2873 square yards on the west side of the Boulevard adjoining St Wilfred's Roman Catholic Church; 700 square yards were bought by the Hull Fishing Vessel Owners for a Fisherlads' Institute. The new School would obviously need more staff and Mr Barnes was appointed full time on £90 from 1910.

The City Architects' Department designed the new School and G. H. Panton & Sons Ltd. won the tender to build it for £5246 in 1912. The tenancy on Harrow Street expired on 1 January 1914. When it opened the new School was the finest School for Fishermen in the country.

In his 1912 report Manton thought that there might be a falling off of attendance as three picture palaces and several boys' clubs had opened in the district, however, attendance over the year actually increased. He also aimed to get more 14-16 year old boys into the School as they could not sign on the crew list of trawlers until they were 16 and even then they had to wait for a favourable opportunity. Apprentices had to attend the School by the terms of their indentures, however, very few did mainly due to overcrowding at the School. The increasing number of apprentices had made the new school essential.

From April 1913 the £1 examination fee was abolished, encouraging more pupils to take the exams. By this time over half the personnel in the fishing industry attended the School and it had the distinction of having presented candidates for the examination of the entire Syllabus and Regulations of the Board of Trade.

Classes began in the new School for Fishermen in January 1914 and the total attendance for 1913/14 was 10,842 for 46 weeks, two weeks less than usual. Manton suggested that to help pay for the upkeep of the School, fishermen should give the price of one cask of livers per annum per vessel. The scheme came into operation after 1919 organised through the Hull Fishing Vessel Owners' Association.

FIRST WORLD WAR

The War had a great effect on the School with the Navy occupying the top floor in 1914. Around 250 - 300 trawlers from Hull were requisitioned in 1914/15 to act as patrols or minesweepers taking away about 2000 potential students. Prize giving was temporarily suspended as half the recipients had been killed. Mr Barnes skippered a mine sweeper in the Dardanelles and was awarded a DSO in 1915.

The School came to the attention of the Admiralty in 1917, they wanted the Fishing Fleet under convoy to have some knowledge of signalling and classes were arranged in the School.

The Admiralty wanted an Admiralty School of Signalling for officers and men of the Mercantile Marine to be established in Hull in 1920. However the Education Committee replied that they did not have the spare accommodation. After representations from the Government the Admiralty was granted permission to appoint an instructor, at their own expense for a class for the Mercantile Marine in the new Nautical School late in 1920. The instructor would also be available, free of charge, to teach signalling to other pupils in the School. However by February 1921 the Admiralty had decided not to go ahead with the scheme.

The average attendance at the School for Fishermen during the War fell from 10,000 in 1914/15 to 6500 for the next three years.

NEW APPRENTICES

A new scheme for employing apprentices on fishing vessels was discussed in 1920 and the Fishing Vessel Owners thought that they should be trained at the Boulevard School and successful apprentices would be guaranteed the position of Boatswain. Riley, the Hull Director of Education, suggested that a Junior Technical Course for boys of 13¼ to 15¼ be set-up. After 15¼ the boys would start their 4 year apprenticeship on seagoing trawlers. Advanced study during their apprenticeship would be at the Technical College. However it was decided to establish a Nautical School, instead of a course, at the Boulevard. The new School opened on the 6 September 1920. Fees were to be paid by adults for the exams, £1 for Mates and £2 for Skippers but there was to be no fee for the Extra Skipper exam.

Riley applied for the school to be recognised as a Nautical School but the Board of Education thought that it better that the School be recognised under the Junior Technical School Regulations.

„ (ADVANCED) ....WEDNESDAY, 8-30 to 9-30 P.M.
ENGLISH (ADVANCED) ....MONDAY, 7-0 to 8-0 P.M.
MATHEMATICS (STAGE II.) ......FRIDAY, 7-15 to 9-30 P.M.
MECHANICS (ELEMENT'RY SOLIDS) TUESD'Y, 7-15 to 8-15 P.M.
CHEMISTRY (ELEMENTARY) FRIDAY, 7-0 to 8-15 P.M. or
SATURDAY 11-30 A.M. to 12-30 P.M.

Instruction for Fishermen.

TEACHER............ R. MANTON (Fisherman).
ST. ANDREW'S HALL, MONDAY & TUESDAY, AT 7-15 P.M.

INSTRUCTION WILL BE GIVEN IN : The use of chart; rule of the road; use of quadrant; how trawls are fixed, showing the use of each piece of net; General Seamanship, as related to navigating the ship to and from sea; the navigation of the Humber; storms, and the necessary precautions to be taken; General Seamanship, as related to towing the gear, and avoiding collision in this respect, and fouling gear, &c.

In addition to the more elementary, teaching, instruction will be given to Fishermen with Skipper's Certificates in decimals, logarithms, trigonometry, navigation, and nautical Astronomy.

The Classes are FREE to Fishermen.

Fig. 67. Prospectus from one of the first classes held in St. Andrew's Hall. (HC)

Mr Manton had to resign in March 1920 due to ill health; he had not been able to attend the School since November 1919. Barnes continued to run the School. When the post was advertised there were 17 replies and from these Charles H. Adamson, of Hull, was appointed Head Master of the Nautical School on £400 per annum from July 1920. He had been a Nautical Instructor on ocean training barques and barquentines. Two assistant masters were also appointed, George Batty and Robert Bennett. Unfortunately Mr Batty died in the August and as there were only 19 students it was decided not to replace him. Robert Bennett resigned in May 1921 to be replaced by J. R. Hoyle in the June.

An extra teacher, S. C. Kemp had to be transferred to the Nautical School in 1921 as there were enough new pupils to form another class. Kemp wanted to be transferred back to an elementary school in 1922 and he was replaced by Harry Edmondson. All the assistant teachers had been recruited from local schools.

An Advisory Committee was setup in December 1920. It consisted of six members, two from the Education Committee, two from the Hull Fishing Vessel Owners' Association and one each from the National Sailors' and Firemen's Union and the National Union of British Fishermen. The new Committee aimed to link the school more closely with the industry.

The Board of Education recommended that instruction in boat pulling should be provided. The Advisory Committee agreed and suggested that Albert Dock should be used. Herbert Dunkerley, Consulting Engineer, presented the School with a suitable boat for boat-pulling in 1923.

THE MERCANTILE MARINE

Adamson thought that Hull did not offer suitable facilities for Mercantile Marine Students who wished to study for the Board of Trade Certificates of Competency for Masters and Mates. There would be ample space in the Boulevard Nautical School to provide instruction and the extra income from fees could be as much as £365 per year. Riley wrote to Hull Trinity House asking for their suggestions. They replied that their school was providing all

necessary training for the Mercantile Marine and that they had plans to extend the school. However, Riley thought that with limited staff and poor equipment Trinity House was not, and could not, supply all the necessary instruction. Trinity House replied further that their staff, although small, were highly trained and the small number of pupils was due to the recession that looked likely to continue for some time. Some 2000 Masters and Officers in the Merchant Service were unemployed in 1921.

A member of the Education Committee suggested the provision of a scheme for Mercantile Marine Engineer Officers, say at the Technical College, in combination with the scheme for navigation officers.

After an inspection of Trinity House Schools a delegation from the Education Committee was impressed by the high standard of work but thought the school had outgrown its present premises. Trinity House said that they planned to erect a new school on Beverley Road whenever the building trade picked-up again. Teachers at Trinity House were

paid less that those at Government schools.

THE END OF FISHING APPRENTICESHIPS

By March 1923 the Hull Fishing Vessel Owner's Association had withdrawn the apprenticeship scheme and recruited crews from casual labour. There was no longer any advantage for a boy attending the Junior School and Riley suggested that the School should train boys solely for the Mercantile Marine as there were currently 44 training for the Mercantile Marine and only 3 for the fishing industry. The Fishing Vessel Owners' protested strongly against the decision. However, boys for the Mercantile Service only were admitted at the Nautical School after April 1923 (skipper and second hand certificates for fishermen continued to be taught).

The Board of Education was prepared to approve the change in status of the Nautical School to one principally concerned with the training of boys for apprenticeship in the mercantile marine from 1924. The Board also stated that from January 1925 every candidate for a Certificate of Competency as Skipper or Second Hand of a fishing boat would have to provide a valid First Aid Certificate. This necessitated the appointment of a Dr Hill to give two lectures per week from November 1924.

All the mercantile marine students were easily found apprenticeships and shipowners would have happily taken more. Adamson suggested that the Education Committee could advertise the School more as teachers and parents did not yet realise that there were two schools at the Boulevard serving different purposes. The public also mistakenly (but not surprisingly) thought that one school was the junior department of the other.

Alfred Holt & Co., Liverpool, (The Blue Funnel Line) accepted a pupil from the Nautical School in 1925. Adamson thought this the most outstanding feature of the Junior Technical School since its inception in 1920 as Holt's only took boys of the highest standard. By July 1926 77 boys were serving in the Mercantile Marine and Humber Pilot Service, 3 in the

Royal Navy and 20 on Hull Steam Trawlers.

A School Magazine appeared in 1923 edited by the English Teacher, Mr Edmondson, who was also Yeoman of Signals.

The old stone 'School for Fishermen' sign over the entrance was supposed to be cut out and replaced by 'Nautical School' in 1923. In view of the expense only a new wooden board was fixed over the old name and painted to match the stonework. The new sign fell off after the school ceased to be used revealing the old stone work that can be seen today.

The change of emphasis from the Fishing Industry to the Mercantile Marine resulted in the adoption, in 1926, of the standard cadet uniform for all students.

Until 1927 there were two classes only - they were referred to as the Seniors and the Juniors. Keen and friendly rivalry existed between the two classes, especially on the football field. The addition of a third class boosted the numbers up to sixty and in the 1930s class entries twice a year produced further growth in spite of a general slump in the fishing in-

dustry. Thus, at the outbreak of the Second World War the school consisted of a Headmaster, five assistant teachers, two part time assistants for Boatwork and Seamanship and one hundred students.

EVACUATION

As in the Great War, the school buildings were given over to service personnel and on 1 September 1939, forty-four of the cadets were evacuated to the Rowntree Quaker School in Scarborough. A few boys remained at the Hull school but by June 1940 more boys were sent to Scarborough and another class was sent to the Axholme district of Lincolnshire. No cadets remained at the Hull School, but because some boys either refused evacuation or couldn't be accommodated, registered numbers fell back to less than seventy. A rearrangement in January 1941 saw the school reunited in classes held at the Whitwood Technical College, Castleford. Attempts were made to restart the school in Hull but severe damage to the premises as a result of enemy action necessitated more cadets being sent out to Whitwood. The cadets were billeted under six different authorities over an area of 150 square miles - each house being visited at monthly intervals by the Welfare Officer, Mrs Edmondson, wife of the master in charge at the time. Increasing billeting difficulties persuaded the authorities to bring all the cadets together under one roof at Wooley Hall, an old Tudor mansion and home of the Wentworth family, midway between Wakefield and Barnsley. With this move Captain Beare returned to take command.

One important consequence of the evacuation to the West Riding was that many local boys were attracted to the school. As a result of this the West Riding LEA granted an unlimited number of scholarships to the Hull school. The strong links forged at the time remained considerable until the 1970s.

In spite of many difficulties, the stay at Wooley Hall was a happy one although the daily 15 mile journey to the Whitwood Tech. was not easily accepted. A more serious problem proved to be the recurring bouts of Scarlet Fever and German Measles that led to periods of complete quarantine. On one occasion the Matron contracted Scarlet Fever, the remainder of the domestic staff went sick except for the Assistant Matron who was left with the task of tending twelve sick boys, one seriously ill with pneumonia. The cooking and domestic chores for the seventy residents had to be completed by the senior master assisted by cadets. November 16, 1943, saw yet another problem when a serious fire broke out in the kitchen at 3 o'clock in the morning. Fortunately, the hall was emptied of all residents in less than five minuets and the Barnsley Fire Brigade arrived just in time to prevent serious damage.

POST WAR

As the danger of serious air attacks passed, the school returned to Hull in the summer of 1944. Numbers were down to about eighty cadets but within two years were restored to their prewar level of over one hundred. It was about this time that the first efforts were made to admit boys of School Certificate standard to the school. Twelve boys were accepted but the experiment had to be dropped the following year because of the lack of applicants.

The 1950s were years of real expansion. Numbers increased at a steady rate and the school buildings had to be extended. The GCE 'O' level examinations were introduced into the school in 1954 and the school curriculum was designed to prepare pupils for these standards in up to seven subjects.

THE COLLEGE

The major post-war developments on the Boulevard campus have concerned the Nautical College that was created as part of the Local Authority's Scheme for Further Education issued in 1948 (the formation of the college had been agreed in 1946). The scheme envisaged a college, separate from the Technical College in which it had previously been housed, capable of providing specialist education for seagoing officers. Five teachers were appointed and the School Headmaster acted as Principal. The seeds of this adult department had been sown in 1931 when a net-mending school was started. Subsequently in 1933 a course for Trawler Engineers began on St Andrew's Dock. These continued except for wartime interference and, with the creation of the new college, they were joined by the first candidates for the Board of Trade Certificate of Competence. A little later the Cookery department was established for catering courses and then in 1950 the radar observer courses commenced and a radar station was set-up on the riverside to the east of St. Andrew's Dock.[6] These latter courses received a tremendous boost in 1960 with the installation of an up-to-date radar simulator at the college, the Hull lecturers assisted in its design. The simulator attracted great attention in Nautical establishments throughout the country and drew visitors from many other countries.

Fig. 68. Prefabs. in the Nautical College Yard, 1950. (KHRO)

The college was situated in two large rooms on the ground floor of the Nautical School. Other notable developments in the college included the setting-up of a Foreign Going Department in prefabricated buildings on the yard in 1946 with examinations for Second Mate, First Mate and Master certificates of competency (the examination centre was on the first floor of Burton's buildings at the corner of Whitefriargate)[7]. At the lower end a one year pre-sea course was started in 1953 for local boys with a good education standard in the hope of raising the academic level of entrants to the Second Mates course; this became a very successful ONC (Nautical Studies) course in 1970. Originally all the boys came from Hull and the East Riding but in 1968 of the 150 cadets most of them came from out of town and lived in lodgings, mainly at the Sailors' Families Association houses at Newland. As the college grew the Fishing section moved to the Hall adjacent to the Catholic Church, next door to the college. Also in the 1950s an Extra Master course was started that tested knowledge, not competency, and Merchant Navy deck officers used it for promotion to the civil service, shipping industry management or teaching. This college expansion put space at a premium and in 1965 plans were announced for a new Nautical College in the centre of the city at an estimated cost of £330,000.

Fig. 69. Former Nautical College, George Street. (RS)

CLOSURE OF THE HIGH SCHOOL

The Nautical School in 1970 was a Secondary High School (the High School for Nautical Training) providing full time education for boys interested in a sea-going career. The wide curriculum covered general, academic and vocational subjects - many of them followed to the GCE 'O' level standard. The school was proud of its practical and outdoor projects and activities, which have long been a vital part of the life of the school.

There were plans for a merger with the Trinity House Navigation School to form a new Secondary High School specialising in general education within the nautical environment with an accent on the culture of the sea. The High School for Nautical Training closed when the Nautical College moved to George St. in 1973 (the adult section of the Trinity House Navigation School had already transferred to the Nautical College in 1972).

NEW PREMISES

The Nautical College moved to new purpose-built premises in George Street, which were occupied by students from 1 January 1973 and officially opened on 19 March 1974. The College was the most modern of its kind in the country with a fully equipped ship's bridge on the roof. On the seventh floor was the radar and simulator training section that had the most advanced equipment of its kind in the world.

On the ground floor was a water area of 40ft by 20ft with current and tidal effects, wave and wind generators. It was used for training about ship handling in the open sea, in buoyed channels and in harbours and docks with radio-controlled ship models providing the student with the practical experience he would otherwise have to wait for until he went to sea.

The College became part of Hull College of Higher Education at the reorganisation in 1976. After the merger a B.Sc. in Fishery Studies was approved in 1981; A B.Sc. Fishery Science course had been run at Plymouth Polytechnic since 1973 with the Hull College servicing the Fishing Technology part of the degree. It gradually 'faded away' as a Nautical College before 1988 and some of the fishing courses were transferred to Grimsby although at least one fishery course was still run at George Street in 1990.

Notes for Chapter Seven

1. This chapter is partly based (mainly from the Second World War) on 'Fifty Years On' (1920-1970) an unpublished work by D. Waxman.

2. D. Waxman, Fifty Years On, High School for Nautical Training, 1970.

3. Minutes of the Technical Instruction Committee, 23 November 1898.

4. Gangway, High School for Nautical Training, January 1968.

5. Minutes of Hull Education Committee, 14 April 1908.

6. G.D.Coates, Hull Nautical College 1946-1976, 1992.

7. Ibid.

THE MUNICIPAL ART SCHOOL

The School of Art at 2 Albion Street became part of the Municipal Technical School from 30 June 1895 and John Herbert Parkyn was appointed as its first Head Master. Parkyn was Senior Assistant Master at the National Training School, South Kensington and had studied in London and Paris. Classes at the new Hull Municipal Art School (it also appears as the Hull Municipal School of Science and Art in Government Inspectors reports) started in September 1896. Initially the classes were small although they quickly increased and attracted students from as far as Brigg and Bridlington. There was a total of 219 students in 1895-96, 97 in day and 122 in evening classes.

After the take-over by Hull Corporation the School became administered by its own subcommittee of the Technical Instruction Committee, which first met on 8 January 1896 and thought J. Parkyn should be in control of the School rather than Dr Riley, the Technical School's

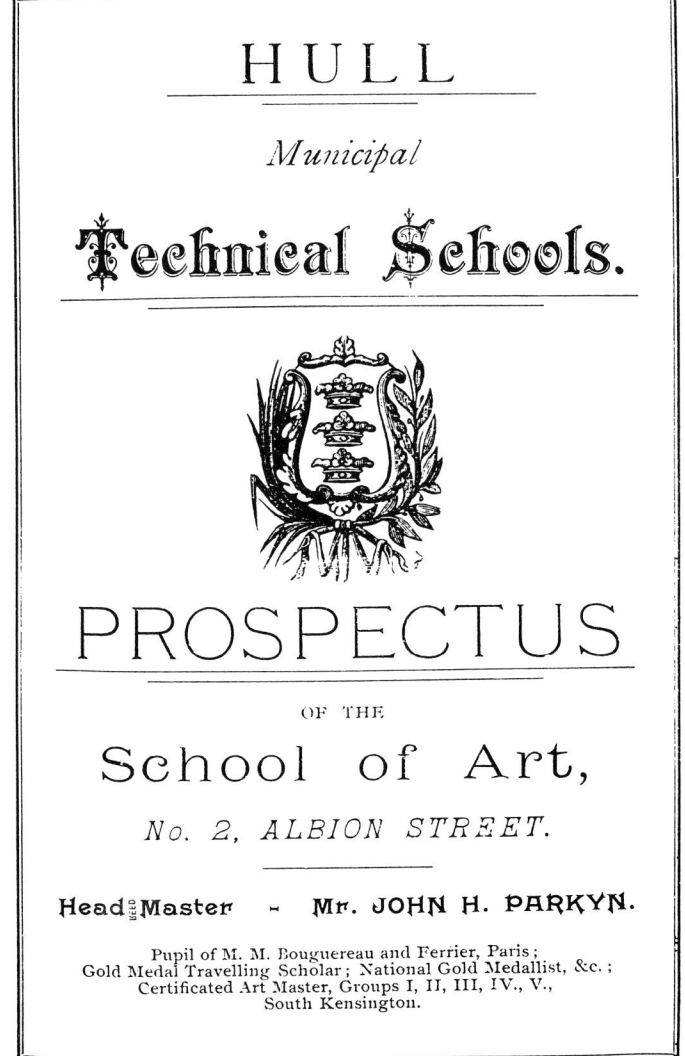

Fig. 70. Frontispiece of first Municipal Art School prospectus (HC)

Fig. 71. Art School, Albion Street. (RH)

lapidated state the Committee decided to repaint the outside but not the interior as the accommodation was only thought to be temporary.

At the end of the first year the Government Inspector's report was very favourable and he asked for the loan of some specimens of students work to show other schools in his circuit. The Inspector also commented that, *"The new Master seems to have introduced a new and vigorous tone into the School, and his efforts appear to be appreciated by the students, as shown by their increased attendance".[1]* To give the students better background knowledge there were nine lecture courses in: anatomy, architecture, historic ornament design, geometry, perspective and memory drawing.

For 1898 the Art Master reported poor attendance of lithographers and architects and that the facilities offered to artisans were not taken full advantage of. There had been very few failures at examinations and a former pupil, Sidney March, now at the Royal College of Art, had been granted both gold and silver medals for modelling the figure.

Director of Studies and Organising Secretary. Parkyn became responsible for the conduct of the School; Dr Riley had been placed in overall charge of the School on take-over.

After an inspection of 2 Albion Street found it in a somewhat di-

The Technical School moved to Park Street in 1898 and John Bilson was appointed architect for the alterations. His original plans would have cost £12,000 including moving the Art School to Park Street. However, the Art School was against the move. *"In view of the proximity of the present School of Art to the Museum and proposed Art Gallery, which are to be taken over by the Technical Instruction Committee, and of the advantage derived therefrom by the students of the School, this Committee is of the view that the Art School should not be removed to the new premises in Park Street."*[2]

Fig. 72. The Art School, Anlaby Road (CJK)

A Science and Art Department inspection of the Art School in 1899 commended the instruction but found serious faults with the building. The rooms were too small, daylight bad and modelling had to be done in a cellar that was damp, ill-ventilated and unsanitary. The inspector had no choice but to recommend that recognition of the Art School be withheld after the present session unless the Council took immediate steps to rehouse it. As a very temporary solution some classes moved to the chemical laboratory in Bond Street.

A NEW ART SCHOOL

The Technical Instruction Committee visited other municipal art schools and found that most had been purpose built and they decided to levy a ¼d in the pound rate to build a new art school. Numerous sites around Albion Street, Kingston Square, Wright and Baker Streets seemed attractive but they all proved to be either unobtainable or unsuitable. Eventually they chose the corner of Jarratt and Bond Street, how-

ever, the Art Master had been on holiday when the decision had been taken and strongly disapproved of the "ugly, square site".[3] This became somewhat academic when the full Hull Council refused to sanction the purchase. Next the Technical Instruction Committee tried for 26 and 27 Albion Street and even produced detailed plans of the new building in 1900, however, the following year a larger site became available. Carr Lane and Anlaby Road were to be widened and the Council had bought property along the route. Initially the Works Committee offered a site in Carr Lane adjoining the North Eastern Railway Company's station yard but NER's conditions for the use of the land proved unacceptable. Next the Works Committee offered 58, 60 and 62 Anlaby Road, however, this site had apparently already been resold to NER. Finally the Technical Instruction Committee acquired 50, 52 and 54 Anlaby Road for £5380, the site contained 1442 sq. yd.

For such an important new building the Technical Instruction Committee decided to hold an architectural competition and appointed Sidney Smith FRIBA to adjudicate the designs. Numerous conditions were placed on the architects including that the building had to be in Renaissance style. A total of 89 drawings were received for the competition and Lanchester, Stewart & Rickards won first prize. Hockney & Liggins won the tender to build the new school and Garth Jones designed the mosaic above the entrance. The Art School was officially opened on 5 October 1905 at a cost of over £13000; although some students had moved in by February 1905.

The inspection of the Art School in 1905 was favourable. *"The Head Master is a trained Art Master of great experience, and is an associate of the Royal College of Art. Under his able direction the school has done exceedingly good work under the most adverse conditions, and the success of the school is largely due to his zealous and unremitting attention.*

The Committee are to be congratulated on now possessing a School of Art in every way worthy of the City."4

Unfortunately J. H. Parkyn had to resign in July 1906 after complaints about his conduct from some past and present female students. He was temporarily replaced by A. W. Turner of York and in the September by George Marples of Huddersfield. One of the new Headmaster's first duties was to set-up a School of Crafts in the Art School.

The Art School moved to new premises on Queen's Gardens in 1974 although the Anlaby Road site was retained as an annexe. After reorganisation in 1976 the School became part of Hull College of Higher Education, now the University of Humberside.

THE ART GALLERY AND THE MUSEUM

In 1897 the Jubilee Committee (Queen Victoria's) suggested the idea of a public art gallery under the control of the Public Libraries Committee, however, that committee had no spare money. The gallery was to be built in the Literary and Philosophical Society's premises in Albion Street, above its museum, by the Society and then leased to the Council. To fund the art gallery the Council decided that if the Technical Instruction (Finance and General Purposes) Committee took over the museum it could then have responsibility for the gallery as well. From 1898 a rate of 1/8d in the pound went to maintain the museum and art gallery. Control of the art gallery then passed to the Technical Instruction (Art) Committee and Parkyn was appointed its first Curator, however, he resigned that post in 1900 to be replaced by A. H. Proctor. B. S. Jacobs was the architect for the gallery and alterations at the museum.

Fig. 73. Plan of Art Gallery, Albion Street, 1898 (KHRO)

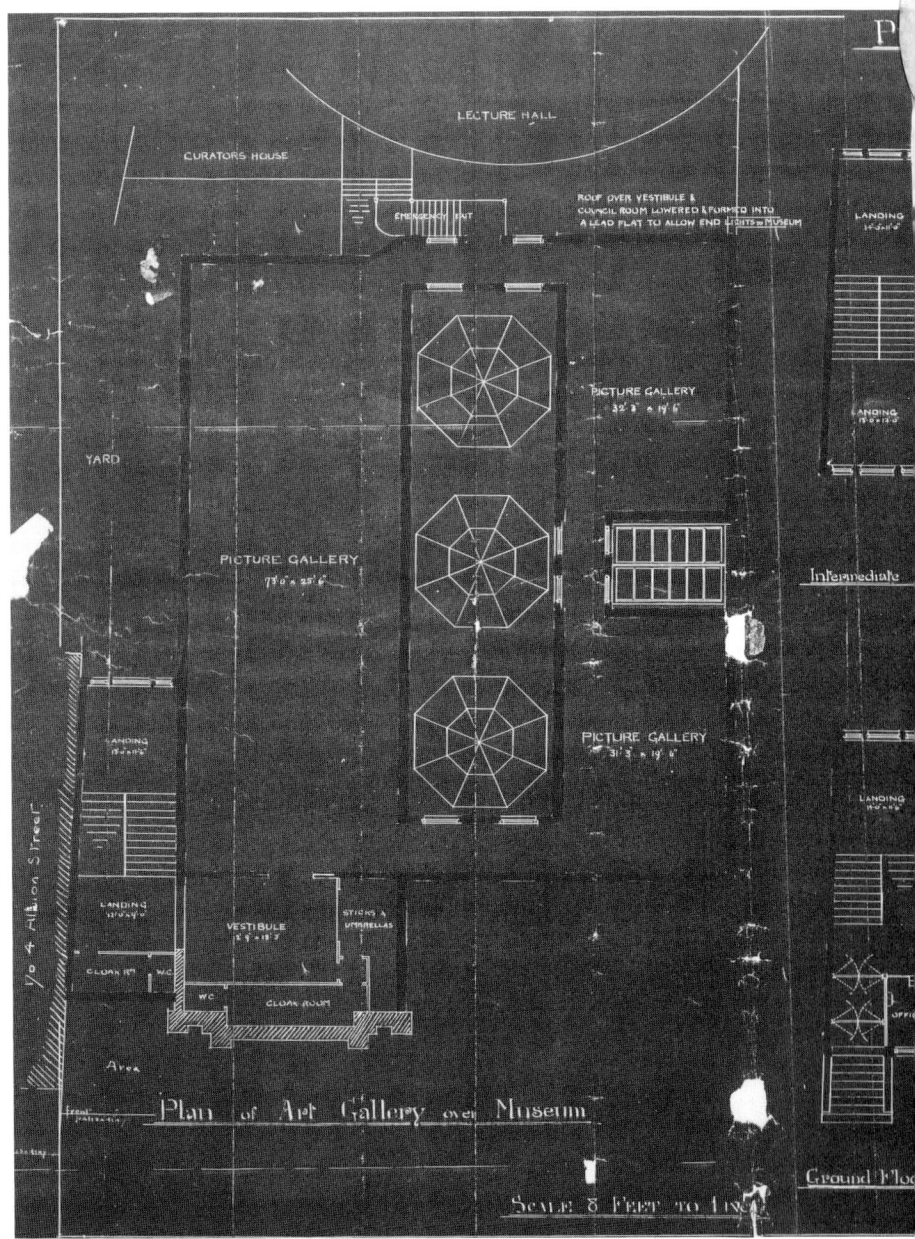

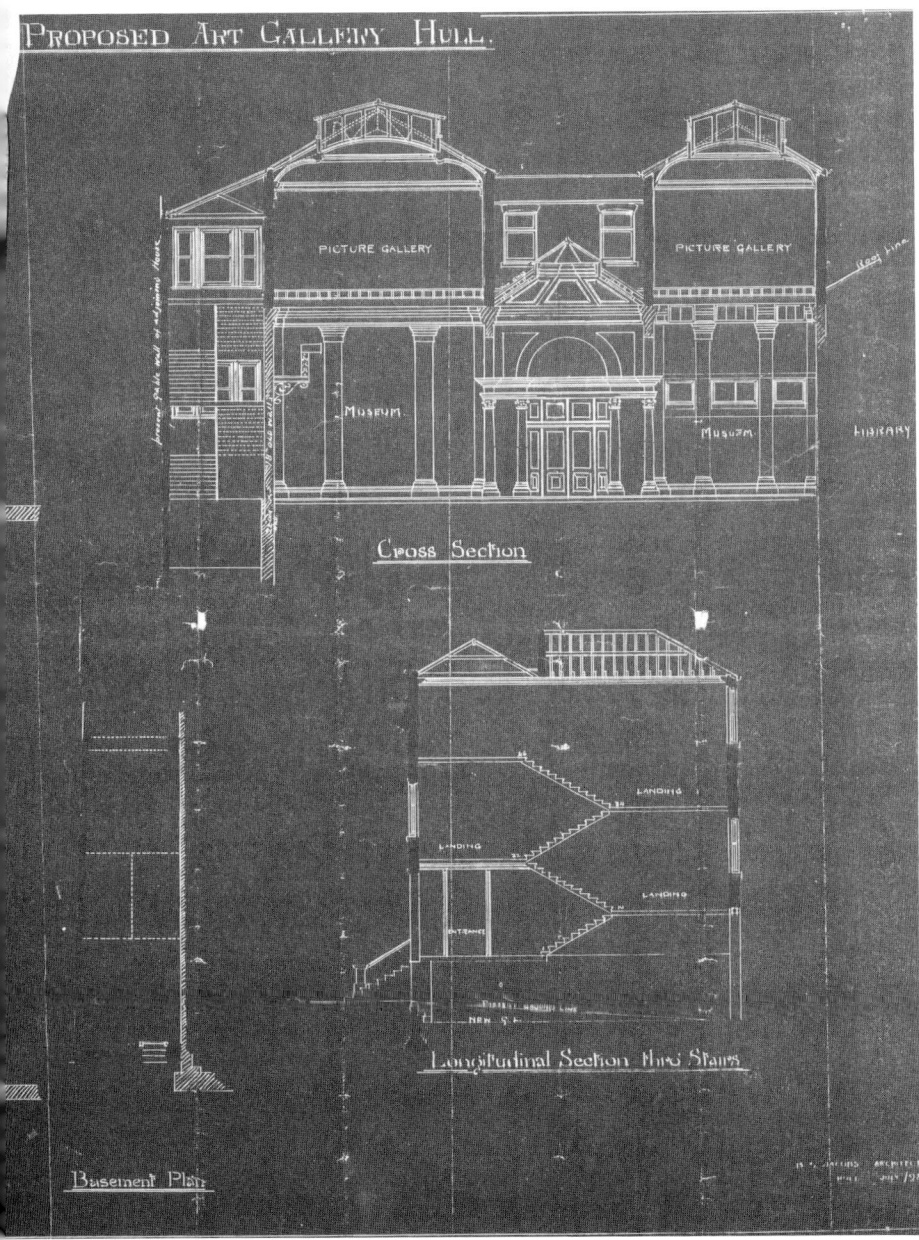

The Art Gallery was officially opened by the Mayor on Tuesday 8 May 1900 with an inaugural exhibition of 482 works by local artists. The exhibition was free except on Wednesdays when visitors had to pay 3d and by the end of its season in late July it had attracted over 30,000 visitors. The autumn exhibition contained more *"great works"*[5] but to loan these proved expensive so a flat entrance fee of 6d had to be charged although the last two weeks were free. The Art School used rooms in the Art Gallery as extra classrooms to great success.

T. R. Ferens, chairman of Reckitt & Son and a local benefactor, gave £1000 a year for five years to buy pictures and he made a similar gift when the new Art Gallery opened in the City Hall in 1910. The third municipal art gallery, opened in 1924 in Queen Victoria Square, was named in honour of Ferens.

Thomas Sheppard was appointed as Curator of the museum by Dr Riley, the Technical School's Director of Studies, and the Chairman of the Committee from February 1901. Control of the museum passed from the Technical Instruction (Finance and General Purposes) Committee to the Technical Instruction (Art) Committee in the June. After alterations the museum reopened on Coronation Day in 1902 and during its first six weeks attracted 15 558 visitors.

The responsibilities of the Technical Instruction Committee now stretched to a technical school, art school, museum and an art gallery, mainly financed by a tax on alcohol.

The Albion Street museum continued to be the main municipal museum in Hull and was of national importance. Unfortunately it was destroyed during the Second World War. The remaining facade was later demolished.

Notes for Chapter Eight

1.   Minutes of the Technical Instruction Committee, 4 December 1897.
2.   Ibid., 12 January 1898.
3.   Ibid., 8 June 1900.
4.   Minutes of Hull Education Committee, 2 August 1906.
5.   Minutes of the Technical Instruction Committee, 10 October 1900.

Index

Index

Index